WORKING WITH WORDS

A Concise Guide for
Media Editors and Writers

WORKING WITH WORDS

A Concise Guide for Media Editors and Writers

Brian S. Brooks
James L. Pinson

University of Missouri School of Journalism

ST. MARTIN'S PRESS   NEW YORK

Senior Editor: Mark Gallaher
Project Editor: Bruce S. Glassman
Production Supervisor: Christine Pearson
Text Design: Leon Bolognese
Cover Art and Design: Ben Santora

Manufactured in the United States of America.
3210
fedcb

For information, write:
St. Martin's Press, Inc.
175 Fifth Avenue
New York, NY 10010

ISBN: 0-312-02673-0
ISBN: 0-312-02067-8

Library of Congress Cataloging-in-Publication Data

Brooks, Brian S.
    Working with words.

    1. Journalism—Authorship. 2. Journalism—Editing.
I. Pinson, James. II. Title.
PN4775.B725 1989   070.4'15   88-29530
ISBN 0-312-02673-0
    0-312-02067-8 (pbk.)

Preface

According to the fifth-century B.C. Indian scholar Panini, author of one of the world's first grammar books, "Who knows my grammar knows God." We won't make the same claim for this book. We will say, though, that anyone who learns the material in "Working with Words" will have a firm grasp of practical grammar, punctuation and usage.

The emphasis here is on the *practical*. As teachers of journalism and editors of a daily newspaper, we were frustrated in finding a single practical grammar and usage handbook that was useful to both students and professionals as a text and a reference.

The AP Stylebook is good as far as it goes, but its intention is not so much to codify grammar as to establish matters of style—what to abbreviate, what to capitalize, how to write numbers and how to punctuate. As a result, additional grammar advice is often needed if one is to deal with everyday language problems.

The AP Stylebook's bibliography lists specific, single references as authorities for matters with which the Stylebook does not deal. But in matters of grammar, the Stylebook lists a number of books that its authors consulted, rather than one single comprehensive official reference. So, journalists and others looking for help with grammar have to glean it haphazardly from what they remember of grade-school grammar texts or from browsing through whatever books they have handy.

The result is lack of consistency. And when one looks for a single, practical, standard grammar and usage guide, one discovers two extremes.

At one end are a number of academic grammar books that seem to be written for linguists with doctoral degrees rather than for students, writers and editors. Such books often deal with highly technical matters of little practical interest to people who want advice about writing correctly and well.

At the other extreme, many books have been written for a popular audience less knowledgeable about writing than most of our students. People who decide to become writers generally do so because they have some aptitude for it, and the errors they make usually are of a slightly higher order than those explained in the mass-audience grammar books (and even in some grammar books supposedly written for professionals). Aspiring writers and professionals are *not* likely to need to be warned against *ain't*, for example, which such books do, but they *are* likely not to know the difference among the commonly used words *although, though* and *while*, which such books seldom discuss.

When we've used the simpler books in class, a few students have found them helpful, but many have said they learned little that they didn't already know or that they thought worth referring to later.

This book originally began as a series of class handouts to help fill the gap between those extremes for newspaper- and magazine-editing students at the University of Missouri. Some of the handouts, such as those that became the grammar chapters in Part One and the AP style summary in Appendix II, were meant to be quick encapsulations of a large amount of material that normally took a good while to learn.

Other handouts, such as those that provided the basis for the lists of misused and confused words in Part Two, were attempts to get into students' hands more practical, concise and complete guides to usage problems than any in print.

Another handout, a list called "One Word, Two Words or Hyphenated?" (unique as far as we know), was given out as a timesaver at the copydesk—eliminating in many cases the lengthy job of checking such words first in The AP Stylebook, then in Webster's New World Dictionary, and then in Webster's Third International, as is the normal practice at newspapers. We've included this list in Appendix I.

Students expressed appreciation, and sometimes former students sent back word from internships or jobs that the materials helped them on qualifying tests or that others on the publications' staffs had photocopied some of the materials to use on the job.

We've expanded those earlier efforts with suggestions from our students and colleagues. We also received helpful advice from several reviewers in the profession (Warren Burkett, University of Texas at Austin; Donna Dickerson, University of South Florida; Samuel V. Kennedy, Newhouse School, Syracuse University; John Mitchell, Newhouse School, Syracuse University; Beverly Pitts, Ball State University; Leslie Polk, University of Kansas; Clifford Rowe, Pacific Lutheran University) and from senior editor Mark Gallaher and project editor Bruce Glassman of St. Martin's Press. We're especially indebted to Jean Gaddy Wilson, author of the most definitive study ever made of salaries for women in journalism, an expert on women in the media and director of a new program at the University of Missouri called New Directions for News, a journalism think tank. She wrote the chapter on sexist and racist language (Chapter 9). Finally, we want to thank our wives, Anne and Susan, who were so patient with us during the preparation of the manuscript.

We hope "Working with Words" will find a place in media writing and editing classes and that it will prove so useful to students and professionals alike that they will want to keep it on their desks alongside their copies of The AP Stylebook and Webster's New World Dictionry. We've found that the materials here enabled us to eliminate a shelf full of other grammar and usage books we used to peruse to look up answers to everyday problems. We think you'll find the same.

BRIAN S. BROOKS

JAMES PINSON

Contents

Contents

Contents

WORKING WITH WORDS

A Concise Guide for
Media Editors and Writers

Part One

THE BASICS OF GRAMMAR

It will be proved to thy face that thou hast men about thee that usually talk of a noun and a verb and such abominable words as no Christian ear can endure to hear.

—WILLIAM SHAKESPEARE,
"II HENRY VI"

Many people share the suspicion of grammar expressed by the rebel in Shakespeare's play. Even writers, for whom a knowledge of grammar should be one of the main skills of the trade, are often wary of studying the subject.

Many writers rely mainly on what sounds right to them rather than on memorizing rules. To a certain extent, that works. But what sounds right is not always right according to the formal rules of grammar. So what? What good is grammar, anyway? Why should we trust it more than our own ear?

THE VALUE OF GRAMMAR

First, let's understand what grammar is. It's the study of the form and structure of words and their arrangement in speech or writing. In this book for media writers and editors, we'll be focusing on the written language rather than the spoken. We assume that most readers will be native speakers of English who learned intuitively as children the rules for speaking the language.

Talking vs. writing

Why isn't that informal knowledge of English enough for writing, as well as speaking? Why don't we just write the way we talk?

1

For one, speech and writing differ in many ways. What *sounds* right in conversation is often ineffective or inappropriate in writing.

In conversation, for example, we can get across a great deal of meaning through tone of voice, pauses, stress and gestures—meaning that would be lost if we merely wrote down the *words* that were said. At the same time, however, the written language offers tools and opportunities that are not available through oral communication. Kurt Vonnegut Jr. points out one advantage:

> This is what I find most encouraging about the writing trades: They allow mediocre people who are patient and industrious to revise their stupidity, to edit themselves into something like intelligence.

We normally speak much more loosely and informally than we would care to have recorded in writing. Although news sources often gripe about being misquoted by journalists, nobody seems to insist that newspapers print all the *uhs, ers*, stammers and false starts that a tape of their words would reveal.

If your writing relies on how you talk rather than on what is considered correct in writing, you're using the wrong tool for the job. Too many things can go wrong. For example, the words you learned by ear may not be what you thought you heard. (Did you really hear that *d* in *supposed to*?) Or the people around you may not have used words in precisely the way that is considered correct in writing. (They may have lacked the education; they may have spoken a regional dialect that differs from standard English; or they simply may have spoken informally.)

Conventions of grammar and usage

When you get down to it, the basic reason for knowing grammar is to communicate better. (The same can be said for knowing the topic we take up in the second part of the book: *usage*, or the meaning and use of particular words.) Knowing the proper relationships between words and how to use them precisely enables us to say what we mean more efficiently. Knowing grammar and usage makes us better writers, better journalists.

An astute reader may notice, however, that some of the rules seem more to be arbitrary conventions than natural guides through illogic and confusion. But one should not undervalue conventions. Conventions represent agreement, and agreement opens doors to communication.

Actually, a bigger problem is the extent to which the advice in any stylebook, dictionary or grammar book does *not* represent such agreement. The fact is—though few know it—not everyone subscribes to the same rules of style, spelling and grammar.

Among journalists, the most widely accepted standards for style are set by The AP Stylebook and the most widely accepted spellings by Webster's New World Dictionary. We have tried to conform as much as possible to those two books. But on matters of grammar and usage, there is no single standard. We have attempted, for the most part, a consensus approach.

Why traditional grammar?

Of the three major current approaches to grammar— traditional, structural and transformational—we have mainly followed the oldest (the traditional), adopting ideas from the others when they were helpful.

Why do we emphasize the traditional approach? Because it's the approach taken by the publishing industry as a whole; because most grammar and usage guides sold to the public in bookstores follow it; because most language columns in the popular press educating the public about language employ it; because it's still the approach taken most often by school foreign-language texts; because dictionaries use its terms to label words (calling *very*, for example, an adverb, not an intensifier); because its terms are also the ones identified by E.D. Hirsch Jr. in his influential book "Cultural Literacy" as the ones literate Americans know; and because it remains, despite the inroads of the structural and transformational approaches in college English classes, the most widely used system.

We do not deny, however, that other grammar systems represent advances in some ways and are better than the traditional approach for certain applications. But, as we said, the publishing world is dominated by traditional grammar, and that is what journalists are expected to know when they take job tests.

Why do publishers prefer traditional grammar? Partly because it's been around longer and is more widely taught. But mainly because publishers—be they newspaper, magazine or book companies—require the prescriptive approach of traditional grammar rather than the descriptive approach of structural grammar. Traditional grammar says, "This way is the right way." Structural grammar says, "Anything is right if commonly said by native speakers." Publishers prefer the consistency of traditional grammar's set rules, though they may have to be amended periodically to reflect changes in the language.

Why is consistency such a concern? Inconsistencies in the style of a newspaper, magazine or book draw attention to themselves when readers should instead be concentrating on the content. Deviations from standard grammar or usage may cause readers to become confused, maybe even to misinterpret what was written. And when readers discover inconsistencies or misuse of words, credibility is undermined as seriously as if a factual error had been made. In fact, if the language is misused, a factual error can be created either on paper or in the reader's mind.

Besides, consistency saves time and money. Without consistency, a writer might add a comma only to see it taken out by an editor and then put back by a proofreader. If we agree on conventions, we can avoid wasting each other's time—and time, as the saying goes, is money.

Grammar and confidence

Even professional writers often lack confidence in their grammar skills. Many people discover that studying practical grammar not only directly improves their ability to express themselves but also gives them greater confidence in their work. Sometimes, just knowing that you have control over the basics enables you to free your mind to concentrate on what's more important—the content and vision of your writing.

Knowing grammar will help you write better and with greater confidence in the accuracy of what you're writing.

AN OVERVIEW OF GRAMMAR TERMINOLOGY

Grammar terms are part of the "shop talk" of people who work with words. Just as sports have terms for what happens on the playing field, so speaking and writing have terms to describe what goes on in an utterance. A writer or editor who does not know grammar terminology is like a football player who does not know words for positions and plays.

But grammar terminology is confusing to many people—it's usually something studied too long ago to be remembered clearly. Most people, however, at least vaguely recall learning *the eight parts of speech: nouns, pronouns, verbs, adjectives, adverbs, prepositions, conjunctions* and *interjections.*

You probably also learned another set of terms called the *parts of a sentence: subject, predicate, predicate complements (predicate nominative and predicate adjective), direct object, indirect object, noun of direct address, appositive, sentence adverb, prepositional phrase, subject of an infinitive* and so on. It's been said that the parts of speech refer to what words *are,* the parts of a sentence refer to what words *do*—that is, how they are used in a sentence.

Then there are the *verbals—infinitives, gerunds* and *participles*—that don't fit well in either category. And, of course, there are the terms for groups of words—*phrases, clauses* and *sentences.*

Separating grammatical terms into these categories helps, but don't feel bad if the groupings don't always make sense to you. For example, if you look closely at the definitions in this book, which are fairly standard ones, you'll see that some of the parts of speech *are* defined by what they *are* but others are defined by what they *do*—just as we define parts of a sentence. Also, if you look in a dictionary, you'll find that many words can be more than one part of speech, depending on how they're used. For example, in the sentence *"The mayor likes jogging," jogging* is a noun. But in the sentence *"The mayor was jogging down the road," jogging* is a verb. And in the sentence *"Jogging down the road, he felt happy," jogging* is an adjective. Confused?

When English grammarians began in the 18th century to write books about the language, they based them on Latin grammar books. "Parts of speech" is really a mistranslation of the Greek for "parts of a sentence." So, the two categories are not really logically separate. Sometimes, it seems more useful to speak of a word in a sentence as a noun but other times as a subject or direct object, so you need to know both sets of terms.

We'll go into more detail later, but it may be helpful to review briefly at the outset the main terms you'll be encountering. You may want to refer to this section if you run into any difficulty as you read the later chapters.

The eight parts of speech

Nouns **name a person, place, thing, idea or quality**:

Susan, Michigan, book, democracy, beauty.

Pronouns **are the most common of the words that take the place of nouns**:

I, you, him, our, it, theirs, one, someone, everybody.

Verbs **tell what a noun or its substitute is doing or being**:

runs, writes, is, seems.

Adjectives **modify nouns or their substitutes—that is, they describe them**:

red balloon, *short* dog, *superior* medicine, *good* girl.

Adverbs **modify verbs, adjectives or other adverbs**:

turning *slowly, extremely* stupid, *quite rarely* seen.

Interjections **express an emotional outburst**:

Gee! Wow! Darn!

Prepositions **show a relationship between the noun that follows (or its substitute) and another word or words in the sentence**:

to school, *after* the fall, *toward* the future, *in spite of* it all.

Conjunctions **connect words to words, phrases to phrases, clauses to clauses or sentences to sentences**:

this *and* that

near the bank *yet* far from here

The package will arrive either today *or* tomorrow.

The country is stronger *since* she was elected.

That was then. *But* today, he had a different story.

Verbals

An *infinitive* is the form of the verb preceded by *to.* It may be used in place of a noun, adjective or adverb:

To surrender now is a disgrace. (noun)

It is a good day *to run*. (adjective modifying noun *day*)

It is disgraceful *to lie*. (adverb modifying adjective *disgraceful*)

A *gerund* is a form of the verb, usually ending in *-ing,* that is used as a noun:

His niece is a state champion in *swimming*. (object of a preposition)

The whole family enjoys *traveling the country*. (gerund phrase acting as a direct object)

A *participle* is a form of the verb, usually ending in *-ing, -ed, -t* or *-en,* that is used as an adjective:

Shouting, the cheerleader ruined his voice. (adjective modifying *cheerleader*)

Add one *beaten* egg. (adjective modifying *egg*)

Finishing a doctoral degree, she found she had little time for romance. (participial phrase acting as an adjective modifying *she*).

Parts of a sentence

A *subject* is the noun or pronoun that is doing the *acting* or *being* in a sentence. To find the subject, ask, "Who?" or "What?" before the verb:

The *Cornhuskers* won the game. (Who won the game? The Cornhuskers.)

The *fee* for freshmen is more this year. (What is more this year? The fee.)

Sometimes, the subject is also called the *simple subject* to distinguish it from the *complete subject*, which is the subject and its modifiers. In the examples above, *the Cornhuskers* is the complete subject of the first sentence, *the fee for freshmen* is the complete subject of the second.

A *predicate* is the verb in a sentence. Sometimes, it is called the *simple predicate* to distinguish it from the *complete predicate*, which is the

verb and its associated words, such as modifiers, objects or complements:

> Two of the candidates *have dropped* from the race. (Simple predicate: *have dropped*; complete predicate: *have dropped from the race*)

> Lathrop is the Republican expected to run in the next election. (simple predicate: *is*; complete predicate: *is the Republican expected to run in the next election*)

A *direct object* is the direct receiver of the action in a sentence. To find the direct object, ask, "Who?" or "What?" *after* the verb:

> The mail carrier brought the *mail*. (The mail carrier brought what? The *mail*.)

> Thank *him* for me. (Thank whom? *Him*.)

A *predicate objective* (objective complement) sometimes follows the direct object and restates it:

> The American public elected him *president*. (direct object: *him*; predicate objective: *president*)

> The proud parents named their daughter *Jordan*. (direct object: *daughter*; predicate objective: *Jordan*)

An *indirect object* is the person or thing to whom or to which, or for whom or for which, the action is done. To tell the difference between an indirect object and a direct object in front of a predicate objective, remember that you can put *to* or *for* in front of an indirect object:

> Read *me* a story. (direct object: *story*; indirect object: *me*)

> We gave *them* the report this morning. (direct object: *report*; indirect object: *them*)

An *object of a preposition* is the noun or pronoun following a preposition:

> In the *movie,* the robots take over the Earth.

> The skidmarks began near this *driveway*.

If the object of the preposition is also acting as the indirect object of the sentence, by convention its role as indirect object takes precedence in labeling it. This may be because usually a prepositional phrase acts as an adjective or adverb, not as a noun or pronoun: In the sentence *"Rogelio recalled for me the events of that day," me* is the object of the preposition *for* but should more precisely be called the indirect object of the sentence.

A *predicate nominative* is a noun or its substitute that follows a linking verb and defines the subject:

> That is the *record*. (linking verb: *is*)
>
> Samuel Clemens became *Mark Twain*. (linking verb: *became*)

A *predicate adjective* is an adjective that follows a linking verb and describes the subject:

> The bridge seems *unsafe*. (linking verb: *seems*)
>
> He was feeling *small*. (linking verb: was *feeling*)

A *noun of direct address* names the person to whom a statement is addressed:

> *Tom*, can you hear me?
>
> Here it is, *Shirley*.

An *appositive* is a word or phrase that follows a noun or one of its substitutes and renames it. Though it acts as an adjective, an appositive could grammatically take the place of the noun it modifies.

> The runner, *Gustav,* sat on the ground doing yoga stretches to warm up.
>
> His house, *the one without a roof,* is for sale.

An *object of a participle* is the noun or its substitute following a participle:

> Kissing her *hand*, he sneezed. (participle: *kissing*)
>
> A blond-haired man was spotted carrying a *gun*. (participle: *carrying*)

An *object of a gerund* is the noun or its substitute following a gerund:

> Playing *golf* with managerial swine left him feeling sullied. (gerund: *playing*)
>
> The witness told Congress he didn't believe in naming *names*. (gerund: *naming*)

A *subject of an infinitive* is the noun or its substitute that comes between the verb and the infinitive:

> The police took *her* to be a modern John Dillinger. (verb: *took*; infinitive: *to be*)

> He thought *her condition* to appear normal. (Verb: *thought*; infinitive: *to appear*)

An *object of an infinitive (infinitive complement)* answers "What?" "Who?" or "Where?" after an infinitive:

> I want you to answer my *question*. (What do I want you to answer?)

> They thought her to be *Jane*. (Who did they think her to be?)

Phrases, clauses and sentences

Phrases are groups of related words that lack either a subject or predicate or both:

> to the restaurant, walking along the beach, as long as my arm.

Clauses are groups of related words that have both a subject and a predicate:

> He wants it all. (independent clause—forms a complete thought)

> because he wants it all (dependent clause—not a complete thought)

Sentences have at least one independent clause and may have any number of dependent clauses. A sentence expresses a complete thought:

> He loves to watch television to relax. (one independent clause)

> She spends most of her time studying, but she sometimes regrets it. (two independent clauses)

> David Letterman's show proved popular despite the fact it was scheduled late at night. (one independent and one dependent clause)

CHAPTER 1

Subjects and Objects: Nouns, Pronouns and Gerunds

A *noun* is the name of a person, place or thing, or an idea or quality.

Sometimes other words—such as *pronouns, gerunds* and *infinitives*—act as nouns. Sometimes entire *phrases* or *clauses* act as a single noun. Any word or group of words that serves in a sentence as a noun is called a *substantive*.

Here are some examples of substantives:

Whatever happens is fine

Finding a job isn't easy

To tell whether such a phrase is acting as a noun, try substituting a pronoun for it. If it makes sense, the phrase is acting as a noun. Examples:

It is fine.

It isn't easy.

The most common substantives, however, are nouns themselves and their main substitute, pronouns.

NOUN AND PRONOUN FORMS

Nouns and pronouns can change their forms in four ways: in *number,* in *gender,* in *person* and in *case*.

Number

Nouns and pronouns can be singular or plural. In most instances, the pronoun itself indicates its number: *I* (singular), *we* (plural); *he, she, it, one* (singular), *they* (plural). *You*, however, stays the same in singular and plural (although there used to be different forms—remember *thou* and *thee* in the King James Bible?).

The rule for making an English noun plural is, in most instances, to add -s to the singular form. But there are some less-common ways, as well:

- The plural of nouns ending in *-ch, -s, -sh, -ss, -tch, -x, -z* or *-zz* is formed by adding *-es*.

- The plural of nouns ending with a consonant followed by a *-y* is generally formed by changing the *-y* to *-i* and adding *-es: try, tries*. If the noun ends with a vowel followed by *-y*, generally the *-y* stays the same and *-s* is added: *day, days*. For proper nouns ending in a consonant followed by a *-y*, the plural is formed by just adding *-s: Kelly, Kellys*.

- The plural of nouns ending in *-fe* or *-lf* is often formed by changing the ending to *-ve* and adding *-s: knife, knives; self, selves; wife, wives; wolf, wolves*. The plurals of some, however, only require adding *-s: roof, roofs; proof, proofs*.

- The plural of nouns ending in *-o* is often formed simply by adding *-s: duos, ghettos, pianos, radios, solos, trios, zeros*. The plurals of many, however, require *-es: heroes, potatoes, tomatoes, tornadoes, volcanoes*.

- The plural of some words is formed using *-en: child, children; ox, oxen; woman, women*. This is a leftover from the Old English tongue (A.D. 450–1066).

- Some singular words from foreign languages maintain the foreign plural: *alumnus* (male singular) becomes *alumni* (plural); *alumna* (female singular) becomes *alumnae* (plural). Similarly, *bacterium* (singular) becomes *bacteria* (plural); *criterion* becomes *criteria; datum* becomes *data; graffito* becomes *graffiti; medium* becomes *media; memorandum* becomes *memoranda; phenomenon* becomes *phenomena;* and *stratum* becomes *strata*. Notice that many people misuse the plural form of some of these for the singular.

- Some words have the same form in plural as in singular: *deer, sheep*.

- The plural of some compound words is formed by adding an *-s* to the end of the first word: *attorneys general, mothers-in-law*.

- The plural of a single letter or numeral is formed by adding *'s: A's, 1's.* The plural of a multiletter word or abbreviation, or of a multidigit number, is formed without the apostrophe: *ABCs, 1980s.*

Gender

Nouns and pronouns can also have different forms for masculine, feminine or neuter. If something has a sexual identity, it is considered to have that gender, masculine or feminine. If not, it is considered to be neuter. Some words that refer to both masculine and feminine (*children*, for example) are considered neuter. This is a simple version of gender compared to many languages, as you will appreciate if you've studied Spanish or French. And the situation in English is getting even easier. Not many English nouns have gender distinctions anymore, and there is a tendency to do away with those that are left.

For example, a woman who writes poetry used to be called a *poetess*, but that is seen as a demeaning term today, and the preferred word is now *poet* for both men and women. Some words have kept the distinction, but even *actress, hostess* and *stewardess* are disappearing—they're being replaced by *actor, host* and *flight attendant.*

By the way, only nouns and pronouns have gender; people are described by sex. Women, for example, are the female sex, not the female gender.

Person

Person is a term easier to understand by example than by explanation. It refers to who or what is speaking, is spoken to or is spoken about. There are three persons, each of which has particular pronoun forms:

first person: I, we

second person: you, you

third person: he, she, it, one, they

Person is clearer to see with pronouns than with nouns because nouns are generally used only in third person. An exception is a *noun of direct address* (a noun denoting to whom a message is directly addressed), which is in second person:

John, would you help, please?

Ladies and gentlemen, the show is about to begin.

Case

Nouns and pronouns change form according to how they are used in a sentence. These forms are called *cases.*

The *nominative case* is used when the noun or pronoun is the subject, predicate nominative or noun of direct address.

The *objective case* is used when the noun or pronoun is the direct object; the indirect object; the object of a preposition, participle, gerund or infinitive; or the subject of the infinitive.

The *possessive case* is used to show ownership or possession (*the girl's doll*) or attribute (*the computer's power*); or when a phrase is turned around with *of* omitted (*freedom's responsibilities*). Some editors insist that the *of* construction be used with inanimate objects that could not really *own* something. So, they would have you write *the power of the computer* and *the responsibilities of freedom.* Such a rule, however, can run into problems with some idioms, such as *a week's pay.* Would anyone write *the pay of a week?*

Personal pronouns have different forms for each case: *I* (nominative), *me* (objective), *my, mine* (possessive); *you* (nominative), *you* (objective), *your, yours* (possessive); *he, she, it, one* (nominative), *him, her, it, one* (objective), *his, her, hers, its, one's* (possessive). In addition, the relative pronoun *who* has three forms: *who* (nominative), *whom* (objective), *whose* (possessive). By the way, *one's* is the only possessive pronoun that uses an apostrophe to show possession. This is a handy rule to remember to separate *its* from *it's,* and *whose* from *who's.*

Nouns, however, have the same form for nominative and objective cases, and change form only in the possessive case.

The rule for forming the possessive case of nouns is to add *'s* to the end of a singular noun, *'* to the end of a plural noun: *a boy's goal, the boys' goals.* Here are some of the exceptions made in AP style:

- Nouns plural in form but singular in meaning add only an apostrophe: *mumps' effects, General Motors' losses.* But in general, when an inanimate object is doing the possessing, it is better to use *of* or *at: the effects of mumps, the losses at General Motors.*

- Nouns the same in singular and plural are treated like singulars: *sheep's wool.*

- Singular *common nouns* (generic names like *tree, child, happiness*) that end in *s* add *'s* unless the next word starts with an *s: a witness's testimony*, but *for goodness' sake*. If the next word starts with an *s* sound, the possessive common noun takes only an apostrophe: *for (appearance', conscience') sake.*

- Singular *proper nouns* (actual, specific names) ending in *s* add only an apostrophe: *Jesus' birth.*

- Compound words add the apostrophe or *'s* to the word nearest the object possessed: *attorney general's* (singular, possessive) *opinion, mothers-in-law's* (plural, possessive) *affection.*

- In case of ownership by two people, either one or two possessives may be used, depending on the sense. Thus: *Mary and Bill's cars* (they own them together, so one apostrophe for the two) but *Mary's and Bill's cars* (they own them separately, so each takes an apostrophe).

- Some words that sound at first like possessives are really part of descriptive phrases. If you can turn the phrase around and insert *for* between the words, it's a *descriptive phrase* and does not need the apostrophe or *'s: citizens band radio* (radio band for citizens), *teachers college* (college for teachers, not one they own), *writers guide* (a guide for writers).

  Sometimes despite this rule, you have to use an *'s* with descriptive phrases because the plural form doesn't end in *s: a children's play, women's college*. Sometimes, too, a phrase can be turned around and *for* inserted, but *of* would work just as well: *teachers salaries*. Does this mean salaries *for* teachers or salaries *of* teachers? Where it could go either way, you may revert to the possessive for clarity. In this particular example, however, you could drop the *s* and avoid the problem: *teacher salaries.*

  Some other exceptions: *baker's dozen, bakers' yeast, confectioners' sugar, nurse's aide, tinker's dam.*

  If the descriptive phrase is used in the name of an organization, use the apostrophe or not according to the organization's preference:

Actors Equity

Ladies' Home Journal

- Some phrases are really only quasi-possessive: *three week's vacation, my money's worth*. It's better to use a hyphenated form instead, when possible: *three-week vacation*.

- Double possessives—such as *a brother of Bill's*—occur only when two conditions are met: The word after *of* cannot be an inanimate object, and the word before *of* must involve only some of the possessions—in this case, *a* brother, not all of them.

USES AND MISUSES OF NOUNS

Some kinds of nouns are particularly troublesome for writers.

Common nouns vs. proper nouns

Most people know that *common nouns* (generic nouns, such as truck or toothpaste) are not capitalized and that *proper nouns* (such as Andrew, Colorado, January) are. Some trade names have become so commonplace, however, that it's easy to forget they are proper nouns. In such cases, the generic term should always be used unless the specific name brand is being singled out. Here's a list of some trade names that are often used incorrectly when the generic term is meant:

BRAND NAME	GENERIC
Adrenalin	adrenaline
Aqua-Lung	underwater breathing apparatus
Band-Aid	adhesive bandage
Coke	cola
Deep Freeze	freezer
Dumpster	trash bin
Fiberglas	fiberglass
Frigidaire	refrigerator
Frisbee	flying disk
Jeep	jeep (for military vehicle), four-wheel drive vehicle
Jell-O	gelatin
Kitty Litter	cat-box filler
Kleenex	tissue
Laetrile	amygdalin
Ping-Pong	pingpong
Quaalude	methaqualone
Scotch tape	cellophane tape

BRAND NAME	GENERIC
Styrofoam	plastic foam
Touch-Tone	push-button dialing
Vaseline	petroleum jelly
Velcro	loop-and-pile fastener
Windbreaker	nylon jacket
Xerox	photocopy

Another problem posed by proper nouns is in the spelling of some particular names. Take, for example, some names of businesses familiar to most of us. The convenience store *7-Eleven* goes counter to the normal AP rule about when to spell out numbers and when to use numerals. *K mart* has no hyphen and a small *m*, but *Wal-Mart* has a hyphen and a large *M. E.I. du Pont de Nemours & Co.* is confusing because of the small *d*'s and the space in *du Pont*. *McDonnell Douglas* is a triple threat: It's McDonnell not McDonald, it has no hyphen, and there's only one *s* in Douglas.

Abstract nouns vs. concrete nouns

Many writers have found it helpful to distinguish between *abstract nouns* (those that name a quality, attribute or idea, such as *beauty, wealth* or *democracy*) and *concrete nouns* (those that name something material, such as *chair, table* or *flower*). They maintain that the greater the number of abstract nouns in your writing, the harder it will be to understand. On the other hand, using concrete nouns makes your writing more involving and easier for the reader to follow. So, instead of writing about poverty in an abstract way, you're more likely to involve a reader by writing about specific people who are poor. The poet William Carlos Williams summed this up in his motto, "No ideas but in things!"

Collective nouns and uncountable nouns

Collective nouns (nouns singular in form but naming a group of things) and *uncountable nouns* (nouns often plural in form but naming a single thing) stump many people when it comes to subject-verb agreement. We discuss these in detail in Chapter 5.

Compound nouns

Compound nouns pose spelling problems because they are so inconsistent. Some are written as two words, some are one word, some are hyphenated. A compound noun generally starts as two words. Then, as the phrase becomes more frequently used, the two words get shoved together as one, perhaps going through a preliminary hyphenated stage. Here are some common examples that suggest how unpredictable compound nouns can be:

ball point pen

car pool

chain saw

coffee maker (but coffeepot)

farmland

hair stylist (but hairstyle)

higher-up

home buyer (but homeowner)

horse racing (but horse-
 trader)

light bulb

meat loaf

mind-set

moviemaker

passer-by

price tag

video game
 (but videocassette
 and videotape)

(For more examples, see "One Word, Two Words or Hyphenated?" in Appendix A, page **191**.)

Sometimes, compound nouns are used where we might expect a possessive. Some examples: *chair leg, sunlight, teachers college*. In the first example, we find it unnecessary to speak of the chair's leg as a possessive. In the second, we have shortened the phrase "the sun's light" into one word. The third example is a case of the often-confused point about descriptive phrases mentioned earlier. (See page **17**.)

Verbal nouns: gerunds and infinitives

Verbal nouns are nouns made from verbs in the form of *gerunds* and *infinitives*. We will discuss gerunds later in this chapter and infinitives in Chapter 2 on verbs.

KINDS OF PRONOUNS

There are eight kinds of pronouns.

Personal pronouns

Personal pronouns refer to antecedents (nouns or pronouns that have appeared earlier in the sentence or in a previous sentence). These pronouns vary their form according to case: *I, you, he, she, it, one, we, they.* They must agree with their antecedent in case, number and gender. (Some grammarians label *it* or *they*—when not referring to people—as *impersonal pronouns.*)

Indefinite pronouns

Indefinite pronouns are used when the antecedent is general or vaguely defined.

Some are always considered singular: *another, anybody, anyone, anything, each, either, every, everybody, everyone, everything, much, neither, nobody, no one, nothing, somebody, someone, something.*

Some are always considered plural: *both, few, many, others, several.*

Some can be singular or plural depending on their use in the sentence: *all, any, more, none, other, some* and *such.* (See the section on subject-verb agreement in Chapter 5, page **73**.)

Demonstrative pronouns

Demonstrative pronouns point to a particular noun or nouns: *that, this, these, those, such.* If they are used in place of the noun (*Who is* **that**?), demonstrative pronouns are classified as pronouns. If they are used to modify a noun (*Who is* **that** *man*?), they are classified as adjectives. (Some personal and indefinite pronouns can serve as adjectives as well.)

Notice that all of these except *such* must agree in number with the antecedent. *This* and *that* are singular and become *these* and *those* in the plural.

Relative pronouns

Relative pronouns are not only pronouns but also connectives between clauses: *who, whom, whose, which, that* (and sometimes *what*). (Also see Chapter 4, page **61**.)

Reflexive pronouns

Reflexive pronouns are used when a noun acts on itself (*I hurt* **myself**). Examples: *myself, yourself, himself, herself, itself; ourselves, yourselves, themselves.* Note that the first- and second-person forms are formed from the possessive case (*my, our, your*) but the third-person forms are formed from the objective case (*him, her, it, them*).

Intensive pronouns

Intensive pronouns have the same form as reflexive pronouns but are used to intensify attention on another noun or pronoun (*I,* **myself,** *will do it*).

Note that the reflexive and intensive forms are only used in a sentence to refer back to a noun or pronoun in the same sentence. The most common violation of this is with *myself* and *me. Myself,* as we said, is correct when used as an intensive pronoun (*I,* **myself,** *am going*) or as a *reflexive pronoun* (*I hurt* **myself**). It is not correct used as a *personal pronoun* (*For Joann and* **myself,** *goodnight* should be changed to *For Joann and* **me,** *goodnight.*). Sportswriter Red Smith said that *myself* is the refuge of idiots taught early that *me* is a dirty word. A simple rule to remember is never use *myself* in a sentence that did not earlier use the word *I.*

Interrogative pronouns

Interrogative pronouns ask questions: *who, whose, whom, which, what. When* is an adverb, not an interrogative pronoun.

Reciprocal pronouns

Reciprocal pronouns are used to complete action between a pair or among a group of people or things: *each other, one another.*

PRONOUN CASE

The pronoun must be in the proper case for the function it serves in the sentence. Here are the most common rules:

Nominative case

If it's the *subject* or *predicate nominative*, the pronoun needs to be in the nominative case:

She is going to the store.

It is *I*.

Compound subjects are all in the nominative case:

She, he and *they* were arrested at the demonstration.

Pronouns in the complete subject introduced by *as well as* are in nominative case, even though they do not influence the number of the verb:

That photographer, as well as *we* reporters, was in the Soviet Union to cover the summit.

Objective case

A pronoun needs to be in the *objective case* if it's the *direct object; indirect object; object of a preposition, participle, gerund or infinitive*; or the *subject of an infinitive*:

Help *her*. (direct object)

She gave *him* a book. (indirect object)

Bill borrowed the bike from *him*. (object of the preposition *from*)

Missing *him,* she wrote a letter. (object of the participle *missing*)

Reading *it* is difficult. (object of the gerund *reading*)

They took *him* to be *me*. (subject of the infinitive to be: *him*; object of the infinitive: *me*)

Possessive case

If the pronoun is possessive, use the possessive case:

This is *your* paper.

Also, use the possessive case when the pronoun is followed by a gerund:

She enjoyed watching *his* (not *him)* dancing.

Some tricky cases of case

One of the most frequent errors of pronoun case occurs in compound objects of a preposition: *between you and* **I**. The correct form is *between you and* **me** because both pronouns are objects of the preposition *between.*

Another common error of pronoun case occurs in compound direct objects. Many people say, *"They invited a friend and I,"* even though they would never say, *"They invited* **I***."* When the object is compound, it doesn't change the fact that the pronoun should be in the objective case: *They invited a friend and* **me.**

A more specialized instance of confusion concerns pronoun case after an infinitive. Not all grammar books agree on this one, but in general, if you have a noun or its substitute between the verb and the infinitive, use objective case after the infinitive; if not, use nominative case. Thus: *He took me to be* **her** (note the *me);* but *I was thought to be* **she** (note the absence of a noun or pronoun between *thought* and *to be).* This at first seems to be an exception to the rule that the object of an infinitive is in objective case. But actually, *thought to be* is functioning here as a linking verb, making the following pronoun a predicate nominative.

Who vs. whom, whoever vs. whomever

Who and *whom,* and *whoever* and *whomever,* pose special problems for many people because *whom* and *whomever* seem to be on the way out in spoken English. Some experts, according to Theodore Bernstein of The New York Times, advocate getting rid of *whom* altogether, and some suggest using *whom* only after a preposition. But the distinction traditionally drawn, and which AP and most editors follow, is to use *who* or *whoever* when the function in the sentence calls for nominative case, *whom* or *whomever* when it calls for objective case.

Here's an easy test: Begin reading the sentence immediately after the point at which you have a choice between *who* or *whom, whoever* or *whomever*. (If the sentence has more than one clause, this will make sure

you are looking at the correct one.) Then, insert *he* or *him, she* or *her,* or *they* or *them* wherever it makes sense. If *he, she* or *they* works best, use *who* or *whoever.* If *him, her* or *them* works best, use *whom* or *whomever.*
Here are a few examples:

Who did you say wrote "The Red and the Black"? (subject of clause, so nominative case: Did you say *he* wrote "The Red and the Black?")

Whoever is going better get ready. (subject of clause, so nominative case: *He* is going.)

To *whom* are you speaking? (object of preposition, so objective case: Are you speaking to *them*?)

Talk with *whomever* you like, and you'll get the same answer. (object of preposition, so objective case: You like *her*.)

Remember that the correct case must reflect the way the pronoun is used in the clause of which it's a part. Look at this sentence:

It can be dangerous to give your phone number to *whoever* asks for it.

Here the preposition *to* would mislead many people into saying or writing *give your phone number to* **whomever**. Actually, though, the pronoun here is the subject of the clause **whoever** *asks for it.* This *entire* dependent clause takes the place of a single noun and acts as the object of the preposition *to.* Using this test, you would correctly choose *whoever* without much fuss because you would start reading the sentence *after* the pronoun choice and insert *he:* **He** *asks for it.*

Here's another tricky one for which you need either to use this rule or to pay close attention to the pronoun's function in the clause:

The police officer asked the witness to point out *whomever* he saw at the scene of the crime.

This time, *whomever* is correct: *He saw* **him** *at the scene of the crime.*

PRONOUN-ANTECEDENT AGREEMENT

A pronoun must agree with its *antecedent* (the noun or pronoun to which it refers) in person (first, second or third), gender (male, female or neuter) and number (singular or plural).

Clear reference

First, make sure the reader can tell which word is the antecedent—and make sure there is one. Repeat the antecedent, if necessary. Example: *The woman spoke loudly because she was hard of hearing—which practically drove her husband crazy.* What drove the man crazy? His wife's loud speaking or her hearing problem? It's unclear what the antecedent of *which* is. Rewriting this sentence, you might substitute *the noise* for *which.*

Here's another example: *Juanita's mother died when she was 30.* Who was 30? Juanita or her mother? If it was Juanita for example, the sentence could be rewritten: *When Juanita was 30, her mother died.*

In his book "Less Than Words Can Say," Professor Richard Mitchell, editor of The Underground Grammarian, cites this sentence from a Department of Transportation manual: "*If a guest becomes intoxicated, take his or her keys and send them home in a taxi.*" Are we to call a cab for the keys or the guest?

One way to avoid confusion with pronouns and their antecedents is to make sure you don't use a pronoun before you introduce the noun to which it refers. For example, the sentence *If she loses the race, Sally will be heartbroken* would be better rewritten as *If Sally loses the race, she will be heartbroken.*

Still, that wouldn't solve the problem of writers confusingly using the same pronoun for different antecedents: *The Senate passed the bill when it voted on it.* Readers would probably understand that sentence, but why make them work at it? Keep your pronoun references as clear as possible.

Person, gender and number

After making sure the pronoun has an obvious antecedent, you need to see that the pronoun and the antecedent agree in person, gender and number.

The main trouble with agreement in person involves the pronoun *one.* When *one* is the antecedent, the pronoun following should be *one* again, not *he* or *you*: **One** *does what* **one** *has to do.*

The trickiest problem with agreement in gender comes after *Neither . . . nor.* Here the pronoun must agree with the number and gender of the noun that follows *nor*: *Neither Frank nor Jennifer would do* **her** *(not* **his or their***) part.*

The most frequent problem with agreement of number between

the pronoun and its antecedent is one that comes unintentionally from common speech and intentionally from clumsy attempts at avoiding sexism. This is the use of the plural *their* to refer to a singular antecedent that could be either male or female. Sure, *A reporter should check* **his** *copy* is sexist, but *A reporter should check* **their** *copy* is ungrammatical. As for *A reporter should check* **his or her (his/her)** *copy*, that gets tiresome fast. Best solution: Make the whole thing plural and write **Reporters** *should check* **their** *copy.*

By the way, if the pronoun is used as the subject of the sentence or clause, it also must agree with the verb in number and person. (See the section on subject-verb agreement in Chapter 5, page **73**.)

Consistency

The person of the pronoun should be consistent throughout the sentence. Watch the pronouns used as subjects, and don't shift them later in the sentence:

As we neared Colorado Springs, you (should be *we*) could see the Rocky Mountains.

GERUNDS

A *gerund* is a form of the verb ending in the present participial form (*-ing*) or sometimes in the past participial form (*-ed, -t*, and so on) and is used in place of a noun:

Fishing is a relaxing way to spend a morning.

She was one of the *neglected.*

He is a *drunk.*

The main usage problem is failing to remember that if a gerund is directly preceded by a pronoun or noun, the pronoun or noun must be in the possessive case: *He's sorry about his* **friends'** *bickering.* Occasionally, however, what you think is a gerund is actually a participle, so this rule may not apply.

Take, for example, this sentence: *Can you imagine (him, his) singing?* The correct pronoun could be either *him* or *his*, depending on what is meant. If the writer is interested in the singing, then *singing* is a gerund and takes *his.* If the writer is more interested in this particular person's abilities, then *singing* is a participle and takes *him*. Say these sentences aloud, emphasizing the italic word, and notice the shift in meaning:

Can you imagine his *singing?*

Can you imagine *him* fat?

How can *singing* be an adjective? Substitute another adjective for the phrase, and it becomes clearer:

Can you imagine him naked?

CHAPTER 2

Verbs

A verb expresses action or state of being. It is the only part of speech that can sometimes stand alone as a complete sentence: *Go!*

Most writers consider verbs the strongest of the parts of speech and the most important to use properly. Look at any piece of effective writing, and you'll see that verbs are what give it life. Verbs are the fuel that powers sentences. Because they're so important, however, there's more to know about them than the other parts of speech. If you start to get bogged down in this chapter, slow your pace, but keep at it. Just remember, this is as steep as it gets; after verbs, grammar is all downhill.

HELPING VERBS VS. MAIN VERBS

To begin, verbs are either *main (principal) verbs* or *helping (auxiliary) verbs*. A main verb may stand alone, or it may have other helping verbs accompanying it.

I *love* my job. (*Love* is the main verb.)

I *have loved* working here. (*Loved* is the main verb, have the helping verb.)

The helping verbs are: *am, are, being, can, could, did, do, does, has, had, have, is, may, might, must, ought, shall, should, was, were, will* and *would*.

Helping verbs are frequently misused in several ways:

- Don't confuse the preposition *of* with the verb *have*: *could have* (not could of); *might have* (not might of); *must have* (not must of); *shall have* (not shall of); *should have* (not should of); *will have* (not will of); *would have* (not would of);

- The helping verb *to have* can also be used to imply volition: *I had my fortune told*. To avoid confusion, don't use a form of *to have* in situations where it might imply volition when none is intended. So, for example, rewrite *He had his arm broken* as *He broke his arm*, and rewrite *He had three passes intercepted* as *Three of his passes were intercepted*. The subject of these sentences did not hire someone to break his arm or to intercept his passes.

- Don't use *would have* with *could have*. Wrong: *If he **would** not **have had** an operation the week before, he could have finished the race.* Right: *If he **had not had** an operation the week before, he could have finished the race.*

- Don't use helping verbs such as *had* or *should* with *ought*. Rewrite *We had ought to leave* or *We'd ought to leave* as *We ought to leave*.

- Some editors insist that the helping verbs be kept next to the main verb in *compound tenses* (tenses that require a helping verb in their formation). For example, these editors would rewrite *She would absolutely like to excel* to keep the adverb from interrupting the parts of the verb: *She absolutely would like to excel*. We have been unable to find any grammar book that agrees with this practice; in fact, Wilson Follett's influential book "Modern American Usage" says of it, "The results are uniformly bad." We would discourage the practice for several reasons, including the fact that it makes for sentences written in a non-conversational order, that the adverb *not* must be placed between the parts of the verb regardless and that changing the order may change the meaning of the sentence. (See the discussion of adverb order in Chapter 3, page **53**.)

In addition, all verbs have seven characteristics: *person, number, tense, tone, voice, mood,* and *transitiveness or intransitiveness.*

PERSON

All verbs have *person*. There is an appropriate verb form for each *personal pronoun* though only the third-person singular usually changes: I *go* (first-person singular); you *go* (second-person singular); he, she, it, one *goes* (third-person singular); we *go* (first-person plural); you *go* (second-person plural); they *go* (third-person plural).

NUMBER

All verbs have *number*. A verb is either singular or plural, corresponding to the number of the subject. Some of the most frequent grammatical mistakes involve tricky situations where people tend to lose track of number between the subject and verb. (See Chapter 5, page **73**.) For now, we'll just point out that in the examples listed under person, the first three forms have singular subjects, and the last three have plural subjects. Although plural nouns usually end in -s, plural verbs do not. In fact, a verb ending in -s is usually the third-person singular form.

TENSE

All verbs have *tense*. Verb tense refers to time—when the action or state of being the verb represents takes place. Chinese verbs are all in the same tense, and the time is indicated by an adverb: *I go today. I go yesterday. I go tomorrow.* In English, however, verbs have a time element built into them, even though an adverb may supply additional details.

Forming the tenses

Different grammarians say there are different numbers of tenses, but we'll discuss six: past, present and future; and past perfect, present perfect and future perfect. As an example, we'll *conjugate* (show the various forms) of the verb *to edit*.

PRESENT TENSE

I edit	we edit
you edit	you edit
he, she, it, one edits	they edit

PAST TENSE

I edited	we edited
you edited	you edited
he, she, it, one edited	they edited

FUTURE TENSE

I shall edit	we shall edit
you will edit	you will edit
he, she, it, one will edit	they will edit

PRESENT-PERFECT TENSE

I have edited	we have edited
you have edited	you have edited
he, she, it, one	they have edited
has edited	

PAST-PERFECT TENSE

I had edited	we had edited
you had edited	you had edited
he, she, it, one	they had edited
had edited	

FUTURE-PERFECT TENSE

I shall have edited	we shall have edited
you will have edited	you will have edited
he, she, it, one will	they will have edited
have edited	

Regular vs. irregular verbs

Most, but not all, verbs form their conjugations as *to edit* does. *Regular (weak) verbs* distinguish the past from the present by adding *-ed*, *-t* or *-en*: *edit, edited; leap, leaped* (or *leapt*). Irregular (strong) *verbs* distinguish the past from the present by changing the middle of the verb: *bring, brought; sing, sang.*

A common mistake with verbs is to use an incorrect *past participle*—the form of the verb used in the perfect tenses. Most often, this occurs with irregular verbs. Here is a list of some of the verbs that pose the most trouble. We have listed the *principal parts* (most-common verb forms) of each: the present, past and past participle forms.

awake, awoke, awaked
bear, bore, borne
bid (to offer), *bid, bid*
bid (to command), *bade, bidden*
   (There's no such word as *bidded*.)
broadcast, broadcast, broadcast
burst, burst, burst
cling, clung, clung
dive, dived, dived (*Dove* is only a bird.)
drink, drank, drunk
drown, drowned, drowned (Don't say a

victim *was drowned* unless an assailant held the person's head under the water.)
flow, flowed, flowed
fly (to soar), *flew, flown*
fly (to hit a baseball high), *flied, flied*
forbid, forbade, forbidden
forsake, forsook, forsaken
get, got, got or *gotten*
hang (to suspend), *hung, hung*
hang (to execute), *hanged, hanged*

hide, hid, hidden
kneel, knelt or kneeled, knelt or
   kneeled
lead, led, led
lie (to recline), lay, lain
lay (to set down), laid, laid
pay, paid, paid
plead, pleaded (not pled), pleaded
prove, proved, proved (Proven is only
   an adjective.)
ring, rang, rung
rise, rose, risen
set (to place down; also: hens set, cement sets and the sun sets), set, set
shake, shook, shaken

shine, shone, shone
show, showed, showed or shown
shrink, shrank, shrunk
sit (to seat oneself), sat, sat
slay, slew, slain
spring, sprang, sprung
steal, stole, stolen
strive, strove, striven
swear, swore, sworn
swim, swam, swum
swing, swung, swung
tread, trod, trodden or trod
wake, woke, waked
weave, wove, woven
wring, wrung, wrung

Sequence of tenses

One of the most important things to remember about verb tenses is to use the right one for what you're trying to say. It's helpful, first, to understand the time order of the tenses. Here they are, listed from furthest back in time to the furthest in the future:

past perfect: events before those described in past tense and
   now concluded
past: events in the past that are now concluded
present perfect: events that started before the present but are
   not concluded
present: now
future perfect: events that will have been completed in the future; usually more speculative than the simple future tense
future: events definitely to occur in the future

Notice that the form is always past, present, future, with the perfect tenses older than the simple ones. This is called the *natural tense progression*.

Once you've selected the proper tense, for the most part you'll want to keep the verb tense consistent. For example, don't start out using *said* to attribute every quotation and then switch later to *says*; pick one or the other (*says* generally for a feature story only) and stick to it.

You *can*, however, switch tense for a reason—such as to go into a flashback. If switching tenses becomes necessary, it is important to follow the correct *sequence of tenses*. The most obvious rule here is that for an event taking place before the time you've been writing about, you need to use a tense earlier in the natural tense progression list.

For example, if you've been writing in present tense and now you want to write about something that took place earlier, you would switch to the present perfect, past or past perfect.

Some editors insist on a special rule governing sequence of tenses in what is called *reported speech*. Under this rule, when one is *paraphrasing* (not directly quoting) what someone has said, present tense becomes past tense (for example, *edit* becomes *edited*, *can* becomes *could* and *may* becomes *might*), past tense becomes past perfect (*edited* becomes *had edited*), and the *shall* or *will* in the future or future perfect tenses becomes *should* or *would*.

For example, someone says, "*I* **am** *young, but I* **am** *wise.*" In reported speech, say editors who support this rule, the sentence should become: *She said she* **was** *young but that she* **was** *wise.*

We think there is an obvious problem with this rule. Notice in the previous example that the meaning has been subtly changed in the reported-speech version. Something that was true *in the present* in the first (direct speech) version is presented in the reported speech version as being true *only in the past*—it may not be true anymore in the present.

Another example: "*I* **will** *speak to the class*" becomes *She said she* **would** *speak to the class.* But we are left wondering whether the speaker in fact *will* do so or only *would* under certain conditions.

Common usage here—*She said she* **is** *young but she* **is** *wise* and *She said she* **will** *speak to the class*—is clearly capable of more nuances of meaning. Pedantry on this point seems to work against clear communication rather than for it, so we urge writers and editors to be flexible. We do not stand alone on this: Traditional grammar books are not so much in agreement on this point as some editors suggest.

TONE

All verbs have *tone*. Tone is a matter of emphasis or stress. Think of the conjugations of a verb in each of the six tenses we listed earlier as the *normal tone* of the verb. In addition to that normal tone, there are three other tones or ways to emphasize the verb in each tense: the *emphatic tone*, the *progressive tone* and the *progressive-emphatic tone*. Understanding how to use and form these tones adds greater range to writers' ability to express shades of meaning.

The *emphatic tone* adds greater emphasis to what is said than the normal tense forms. It is formed in one of three ways for each tense: by adding a form of the verb *to do* as a helping verb, by underlining or italicizing the helping verb, or by changing *shall* to *will* and *will* to *shall*. Here's a demonstration:

Present emphatic: I *do* edit, he *does* edit

Past emphatic: I *did* edit

Future emphatic: I *will* edit, you *shall* edit

Present-perfect emphatic: I *have* edited, he *has* edited

Past-perfect emphatic: I *had* edited

Future-perfect emphatic: I *will have* edited, you *shall have* edited

The *progressive tone* stresses the ongoingness of the verb. It's formed by using a form of the verb *to be* as a helping verb in front of the *present participle* (the form of the verb ending in *-ing*):

Present progressive: I *am* editing, you *are* editing, he *is* editing

Past progressive: I *was* editing, you *were* editing

Future progressive: I *shall be* editing, you *will be* editing

Present-perfect progressive: I *have been* editing, he *has been* editing

Past-perfect progressive: I *had been* editing

Future-perfect progressive: I *shall have been* editing, you *will have been* editing

The *progressive-emphatic tone* both emphasizes the verb and stresses its ongoingness. This tone is formed by either underlining or italicizing the progressive-tone form or by changing *shall* to *will* and *will* to *shall*:

Present-progressive emphatic: I *am* editing, you *are* editing, he *is* editing

Past-progressive emphatic: I *was* editing, you *were* editing

Future-progressive emphatic: I *will be* editing, you *shall be* editing

Present-perfect-progressive emphatic: I *have been* editing, he *has* been editing

Past-perfect-progressive emphatic: I *had* been editing

Future-perfect-progressive emphatic: I *will have been* editing, you *shall have been* editing

VOICE

All verbs are either in the *active voice* or in the *passive voice*. Active voice emphasizes the doer of an action by making it the subject of the sentence: **Jill** *hit the ball*. Passive voice emphasizes the receiver of an action by making it the subject of the sentence: *The* **ball** *was hit by Jill*. The direct object of the active-voice sentence (*ball*) became the subject of the passive-voice sentence.

The passive voice has three characteristics:

- It uses some form of the verb *to be*.
- It uses a participle of the main verb.
- The word *by* or *for* is either present or implied.

The conjugations we listed earlier are all in the active voice. Here are sample conjugations in passive voice:

Present tense, passive voice: I *am* edited, you *are* edited, he *is* edited

Past tense, passive voice: I *was* edited, you *were* edited

Future tense, passive voice: I *shall be* edited, you *will be* edited

Present perfect, passive voice: I *have been* edited, he *has been* edited

Past perfect, passive voice: I *had been* edited

Future perfect, passive voice: I *shall have been* edited, you *will have been* edited

The main thing to remember about passive voice is to avoid using it because it's too wordy, the emphasis is not on the actor, and it's easy to drop the *by* or *for* phrase and not tell who's doing the acting:

The documents were shredded.

Language critic Richard Mitchell calls sentences such as that examples of ''the divine passive''—only God knows who did it.

Good writers rewrite passive-voice sentences in active voice unless they have a specific reason not to do so, such as when the action or the subject being acted upon is more important than the actor. For example, in an accident story, we might find a sentence such as this: *Renfrew was taken to St. Mary's Hospital, where he was listed in critical condition.* That sentence contains two examples of the correct use of the passive voice. Renfrew, the accident victim, is of more importance to the account than either the ambulance attendants who took him to the hospital or the doctor who reported his condition.

Sometimes, writers waste time trying to rewrite what they think are passive-voice sentences that are not. The usual culprit is a sentence with a linking verb and a participle used as an adjective: *The cost was hidden.* At first, this sentence seems to meet all the requirements of passive voice. You can even imagine an implied *by.* But here, the participle is used as an adjective, not as part of the verb. How can you tell? If you can put the word *very* in front of the participle, then it's being used as an adjective, not as a verb. There's no need to rewrite the sentence.

Also, some verbs should normally be used in passive voice. The verb *divorce* must always be passive voice or transitive:

They were divorced. (passive)

He divorced her. (transitive)

Do not write *They married then divorced* or *They separated and later divorced.*

Many purists also insist that the verb *graduate* should be used in the passive voice, as in *She was graduated from the University of Arizona.* The AP Stylebook, however, says that the active voice, *She graduated from the University of Arizona,* is better. In the latter case, though, don't forget the *from.*

MOOD

All verbs have *mood.* Verb mood has to do with how the speaker or writer regards the statement being made. There are four moods: the *indicative,* the *imperative,* the *conditional* and the *subjunctive.*

Indicative mood

We would guess that 90 percent of English sentences are in the indicative mood, meaning the sentence in which the verb appears either states a fact or asks a question. All of the verb conjugations listed earlier were in the indicative mood.

Imperative mood

Some verbs are in the imperative mood, meaning the sentence makes a command or an entreaty or issues instructions:

Do it.

Let's do it.

Please do it.

First, connect part A to part B.

Learning the conjugations of imperative-mood verbs is easy because there is only one verb tense (present) and only two conjugations:

Edit! (second-person singular or plural)

Let's edit! (first-person plural)

Conditional mood

Some sentences use the conditional mood, which as the name implies is used to express a condition. The conditional mood is always represented by one of four helping verbs in English. In the conditional:

can becomes *could*

may becomes *might*

shall becomes *should*

will becomes *would*

If you compare the two forms above of each verb, you'll quickly see the difference. In each case, the first verb expresses greater certainty than the second. (This may not be as apparent in the case of *may* and *might* as the others, but many grammarians would tell you that when these two words are used properly—as they often aren't in conversation—the rule holds with them, as well.) *The law* **will** *close tax loopholes* is more definite than *The bill* **would** *close tax loopholes*. The conditional form is required with the last sentence because a bill is not yet a law—it *would* close tax loopholes if it were passed into law.

Subjunctive mood

Notice in the last sentence that we said "if it *were* (not *was*) passed into law." The *were* is in the fourth mood, *the subjunctive*, which is often used after *if* in sentences in which the verb in the main clause is in the *conditional*. But the *subjunctive mood* doesn't have to follow *if*. It should be used to talk about any condition contrary to fact, such as a wish, a doubt, a prayer, a desire, a request or a hope. (Don't be confused: It may be a fact that I wish something, but *what* I wish for has not yet become true, or I wouldn't be wishing for it.)

Nobody seems to have much trouble with the indicative or imperative moods, or with the conditional for that matter (except for *may* and *might*). The subjunctive, however, is not used nearly so often in English, and few people know how to use it correctly.

Here are some examples of use of the subjunctive:

If I *were* you (but I'm not), I'd quit.

I wish I *were* a cowboy (but I'm not).

The hijackers demanded that 17 terrorists *be* set free (who had not yet been freed).

The first two sentences may sound odd because many people say only *I* **was**, the indicative mood form, even when the subjunctive form is needed. As for the third example, most people would probably correctly use *be* because it sounds right and not even realize they were using the subjunctive.

First, let's learn the conjugations in the subjunctive—they're easy—then look more closely at how this mood is used. The conjugations are not difficult to learn because for most verbs they differ from the indicative in only one tense.

The *present tense of the subjunctive mood* is the infinitive minus the *to*. For all verbs other than *to be* (I be, we be; you be, you be; he, she, it, one be, they be), this differs from the present tense of the indicative mood only in the third-person singular: *He asked that the editor* **edit** *(not* **edits***) his story carefully for potential libel.*

I edit	we edit
you edit	you edit
he, she, it, one edit	they edit

The past-tense subjunctive form of the verb *to be* is in each instance *were*. This is important to remember because some of the most common mistakes using (or not using) the subjunctive involve the verb *to be*. Notice that in the indicative mood, the first- and third-person singular forms would use *was*, but the subjunctive calls for *were*: *If I* **were** *you . . . If she* **were** *taller . . .*

All other tenses and progressives are the same in the subjunctive as in the indicative. So, we often use the subjunctive without realizing it. But that also explains why, in the few cases in which the two moods differ, people often incorrectly use the indicative for the subjunctive: They're not used to making the distinctions anywhere else.

Here is a list of places in which to use the subjunctive:

- Use the subjunctive in most dependent clauses beginning with *if*. *If* usually introduces a condition contrary to fact, so the subjunctive is needed. But occasionally, the condition is not contrary to fact—if the condition is either true or non-committal, as in this sentence, then the indicative is required. The difference can sometimes be tricky.

    Here are some sentences in which *if* introduces a condition contrary to fact, so the subjunctive is used:

    If she **were** *rich (but she's not), she would quit her job.*
    I could attend the class if it **were** *offered sooner (but it's not).*
    If compassion **be** *a crime, then judge me guilty.* (The speaker does not really believe compassion should be considered a crime.)

    Here, on the other hand, are some sentences in which *if* introduces a condition that is either true or about which the speaker is non-committal as to truth or falsity. In these, the indicative has been used:

    If this experiment **works,** *then I will be famous.* (It may or may not work—it is not clearly false.)
    He must have found a ride home if he **is** *not in his office.* (A person

might say this after hearing the fact that a colleague was no longer in his office.)

- If the verb in the main clause is in the indicative mood, then the verb in the dependent clause should also be in the indicative. But if the verb in the main clause is in the *conditional*, then the verb in the dependent clause is usually in the subjunctive:

  I **could** *do it* **were** *I given the proper tools.* (**Could** is conditional, *were* subjunctive.)

- Use the subjunctive in dependent clauses after verbs requiring *that* when the suggestion following is contrary to fact at present: *advise that, anxious that, ask that, demand that, doubt that, eager that, forbid that, hope that, insist that, move that, pray that, prefer that, propose that, recommend that, request that, require that, rule that, suggest that* and *urge that.* Examples:

  I demand that he **stay.**
  I insist that he **go.**
  It is necessary that I **be** *left alone.*

  By contrast, verbs requiring *that* but not implying a condition contrary to present reality do not necessitate the subjunctive: *believe that, conclude that, guess that, imply that, infer that, know that, notice that, say that, suppose that, think that* and *wonder that.*

- Use the subjunctive after *as if* or *as though*: *He sings as though he* **were** *a professional.*

- Use the subjunctive in these idioms: *be it said, be that as it may, come Monday, come what may, far be it (for, from) me, God be with you (God bless, God forbid), lest he forget, long live (the king), so be it, suffice it to say* and *would that I were.*

TRANSITIVENESS VS. INTRANSITIVENESS

All verbs are either *transitive* or *intransitive* in any given sentence. Some are transitive in one sentence but intransitive in another. Verbs are transitive when they have a *direct object* (a receiver of the action) behind them to tell to what or to whom the action was done:

The Legislature *passed* the bill. (Passed what? Passed the bill.)

Police *arrested* Fred Wilson. (Arrested whom? Arrested Fred Wilson.)

Intransitive verbs do not take a direct object. There are two kinds of intransitive verbs: *linking (copulative) verbs* and *complete verbs*.

Linking verbs take a *predicate complement*—either a *predicate nominative* (noun or pronoun behind the linking verb) or a *predicate adjective* (adjective behind the linking verb).

She is a *cabdriver*. (predicate nominative)

This is *she*. (predicate nominative)

He is *tall*. (predicate adjective)

He is *impressed*. (predicate adjective)

A linking verb can be thought of as an equals sign indicating an equation between the subject and the complement. Linking verbs *link* the subject and the subject complement.

Linking verbs must be followed either by a noun or pronoun, or by an adjective. They may also be followed by an adverb but always in combination with an adjective, noun or pronoun:

He said he often was hungry. (*Was* is a linking verb, *hungry* a predicate adjective and *often* an adverb modifying was.)

The list of linking verbs includes the *to be* verbs—*am, is, are, was, were, has been, have been, had been, shall be, will be*; verbs having to do with the five senses—*appear, feel, look, smell, sound, taste*; and these additional verbs—*act, become, continue, grow, remain, seem, stay, turn, wax*. Knowing when a verb is a linking verb helps you deal with troublesome choices between adjectives and adverbs, such as whether a person feels *good* or feels *well*. (See Chapter 3, page **44**.)

***Complete verbs* take neither a direct object nor a predicate complement.**

The woman hesitated.

USES AND MISUSES OF VERBS

Agreement

Make sure the subject and verb agree in person and number. (See Chapter 5, page *73*.)

Consistency

Verb consistency is required to avoid needlessly confusing the readers. Note the following rules:

- The verb tense should be consistent, except for flashbacks or flashforwards. Tense often becomes a problem for journalists when writing photo captions. Captions usually are written in present tense, but sometimes this results in awkwardness: *Two thousand protesters gather in Washington last week, where 300 are arrested.* You could rewrite it: *Two thousand protesters gather in Washington last week, where 300 were arrested,* but now we've shifted tense, and a reader might wonder when those 300 were arrested. Were they arrested before the 2,000 arrived or after? One solution would be to rewrite it in past tense throughout, cut *where* and make two sentences instead of one: *Two thousand protesters gathered in Washington last week. Three hundred were arrested.*

- The voice of the verb should be consistent. Don't needlessly shift from active to passive voice. Example: *Stan Smith loves tennis, and his spare time is devoted to it.* The first clause is in active voice, the second in passive.

- The mood of the verb should be consistent. Some people mistakenly violate this rule in commands: *Read the book, and then you should complete the exercises.* Here, the first clause is in imperative mood, the second in conditional. Rewrite it: *Read the book, then complete the exercises* or *You should read the book, and then you should complete the exercises.*

Nouns used as verbs

Many editors object to using these nouns as verbs:

author (change to *write*)
contact (change to *call, write, visit*)
critique (change to *criticize*)
debut (change to *have its debut*)
gift (change to *give*)
is headquartered (change to *has headquarters in*)
host (change to *hold*)
impact (change to *affect*)
ink (change to *sign*)
interface (change to *interact*)

jet (change to *fly*)
language (change to *speak, write*)
parent (change to *raise*)
pastor (change to *lead a congregation*)
pen (change to *sign*)
premiere (change to *have its premiere*)
process (rewrite; example: change *process words* to *write*)
source (change to *start, inspire, cause*)
target (change to *aim at*)

41

VERBALS

Sometimes, forms of a verb are used as parts of speech other than a verb. These forms are called *verbals*, and there are three kinds: *gerunds, participles* and *infinitives*.

Gerunds

Gerunds are the present or past participial forms of the verb used as a noun. (We discussed these in Chapter 1, page **25**.)

Participles

Participles are the present or past participial forms of the verb used as an adjective. (We'll discuss these in Chapter 3, page **50**.)

Infinitives

Infinitives are the form of the verbs that normally has *to* in front of it, though sometimes the *to* can be omitted: *May I help* **cook**?

Although *to* usually is a *preposition*, this is not true when the word is part of an infinitive. When *to* is followed by a verb, the construction is an infinitive, not a prepositional phrase.

Infinitives may be used as nouns (**To eat** *is* **to live**), adjectives (*The issue* **to be argued** *is a complex one*) or adverbs (*He went* **to visit** *his mother*). Infinitives usually act as nouns or adjectives in intransitive sentences, adverbs in transitive ones.

The biggest question regarding infinitives is whether they can be split. Because Latin infinitives are one word, the grammarians who wrote the first grammars of English in the 18th century decided that English infinitives should not be split. So the rule most editors insist on is don't split infinitives. For example, instead of *She would like* **to quickly make** *her mark* write *She would like* **to make** *her mark quickly*. Instead of *She wants* **to not be** *disturbed* write *She wants* **not to be** *disturbed*.

Actually, however, people split infinitives all the time in conversation, and split infinitives had long been a feature of the language when grammarians invented the rule. Sometimes it's almost impossible to say what we want without splitting infinitives. Humorist James Thurber was adamant on this point: *"When I split an infinitive, it's going* **to** *damn well* **stay** *split.''* Many grammarians now agree and allow latitude when there is no alternative that doesn't sound stilted, when a writer wants **to** *strongly* **emphasize** a point or when a writer is imitating conversation.

Another problem with infinitives involves pronoun case after expressions such as *believed to be* or *thought to be*. We discussed this problem in Chapter 1, page **22**.

Sometimes writers use an *infinitive phrase* as an adjective at the beginning of a sentence but forget that it must modify the next noun or pronoun following it. The result is a *dangling infinitive:* **To get ahead in this business,** *the audience must be kept in mind.* In this example, the phrase *to get ahead in this business* modifies *the audience*, but no doubt the writer meant it to modify *you*, a word that never appears in the sentence. A reader may be able to figure it out, but a dangling infinitive makes the going tougher.

One more problem with infinitives: Don't confuse the conjunction *and* with the word *to* in an infinitive. Many people substitute *and* for *to* in infinitives preceded by *try* or *come*. So, for example, they'll write, *I'll try* **and** *do it* or *He'll come* **and** *work*. Although the respected British poet John Milton used the idiom *try and* as early as 1526, most editors seem to think the phrase a modern illiteracy and insist you write *try to*.

CHAPTER 3

Modifiers: Adjectives, Adverbs, Participles and Interjections

Adjectives and *adverbs* are the main types of modifiers (words that describe or delimit other words). Adjectives modify a noun or its equivalent by telling how many, what kind, which or whose. Adverbs modify a verb, adjective or another adverb; in addition to these main uses, an adverb may modify a verbal, preposition, conjunction, substantive or clause. Adverbs generally tell how, when, where, to what degree or extent, or how much.

Participles are verb forms typically ending in *-ing, -ed, -t* or *-en* that are used in place of an adjective. *Interjections* are used to modify an entire sentence.

COMPARATIVE FORMS OF ADJECTIVES AND ADVERBS

Adjectives and adverbs have *three degrees of comparison*: the *positive*, the *comparative* and the *superlative* forms. (Participles and interjections do not have comparative forms. Some kinds of adjectives and adverbs do not have comparative forms either.)

The positive is the base form of an adjective or adverb and implies no comparison. The comparative is used in comparisons of two items or two groups. The superlative is used in comparisons involving more than two items or groups.

For most short adjectives, add *-er* or *less* to the positive form to make the comparative and *-est* or *least* to make the superlative:

tall (positive)

taller or less tall (comparative)

tallest or least tall (superlative)

For most longer adjectives, add the words *more* or *less* in front of the positive form to make the comparative and *most* or *least* in front of the positive to make the superlative:

beautiful (positive)

more beautiful or less beautiful (comparative)

most beautiful or least beautiful (superlative)

Two main exceptions are *good, better* and *best*; and *bad, worse* and *worst*.

Most adverbs are formed by adding *-ly* to the end of the positive form of an adjective. This *-ly* form is then the positive form of the adverb. The comparative form is made by putting the word *more* or *less* in front of the positive form, and the superlative form is made by putting the word *most* or *least* in front of the positive form:

quick (adjective)

quickly (positive form of the adverb)

more or less quickly (comparative forms of the adverb)

most or least quickly (superlative forms of the adverb)

The degrees of comparison give some writers problems. One of the most frequent problems is misusing the comparative when the superlative is called for or vice versa. For example, many writers will list a number of items, then refer to *the latter one*. But *latter*, like *former*, should be used only when two items have been listed because they are comparative, not superlative, forms. *Last* and *first* are called for instead in such cases.

On the other hand, don't say someone is *the **oldest** of the two brothers*. If there are only two, he's the *older*.

Another problem involves what to include in comparisons. Example: *The new reporter is **faster than anyone** on the staff.* Assuming the new reporter is also on the staff, then he or she cannot be faster than anyone on the staff because the staff includes this reporter. The sentence should be rewritten: *The new reporter is **faster than anyone else** on the staff.*

Yet another common problem is that some adjectives and adverbs don't have comparative and superlative forms. They name something absolute that doesn't have any degrees. Something cannot be *more unique* than something else because unique means one of a kind. Something is either one of a kind or it isn't.

Likewise, something cannot be *most unique, rather unique, somewhat unique* or *very unique*. Another word that should not be used with comparatives is *perfect*, contrary to the Preamble to the Constitution's famous phrase "in order to form a more perfect union."

Other words lacking comparative and superlative forms include the adjectives *dead, endless, perpendicular, square* and *straight*, and the adverb *especially*. It is permissible to use these with comparative forms when they are not used in their literal sense: *That was the **deadest** class I've ever taken.*

KINDS OF ADJECTIVES

There are three main kinds of adjectives, *attributive adjectives, predicate adjectives* and *determiners*, labeled according to their relationships to the nouns or pronouns they modify.

Attributive adjectives

Attributive adjectives may either directly precede or directly follow the words they modify:

the *handsome* man

the man, *tall* and *handsome*

Predicate adjectives

Predicate adjectives follow a linking verb and refer back to the subject:

The man is *handsome.*

Don't confuse a predicate adjective with an adverb. Linking verbs—such as *appear, be, become, feel, grow, look, seem, smell, sound* and *taste*—generally take a predicate adjective rather than an adverb (see Chapter 2, page **40**).

Some intransitive verbs are confusing because in some uses they may be linking verbs and take a predicate adjective but in others they may be complete and be followed by an adverb. Look at these examples:

He feels *good* to be alive. (linking verb with predicate adjective modifying the subject *he*)

One's finger cannot feel *well* with heavy gloves on. (adverb modifying the complete verb *feel*)

The patient feels *well* enough to be discharged. (linking verb with predicate adjective modifying the subject *patient*)

Good is an adjective, so you use it after a linking verb to describe the spirits of the *subject*. If you want to describe the action of feeling (touching), the verb rather than the subject, then you should use the adverb *well*. Of course, *well* can also be used as an adjective to mean the opposite of *ill*. So you must use *well* (adverb) if you're describing one's ability to feel, *good* (adjective) for someone's mood or *well* (adjective) for someone's health.

Consider this sentence: *The thunder sounded (loud or loudly).* To decide between an adjective or an adverb, ask yourself whether the subject is acting. If the sentence means the thunder *clapped* (acted), then it clapped *loudly* (adverb). If it means the thunder *was* (being) loud, then the thunder sounded *loud* (adjective).

So a flower smells *sweet* not *sweetly* because the flower is not acting, just being—it has no nose with which to smell. Likewise, you wax (linking verb) *poetic*, but you wax (transitive verb) *carefully* your car.

Determiners

Structural grammar books speak of another category of adjectives called *determiners*. These are all attributive adjectives in that they precede the noun or pronoun they modify, but unlike normal adjectives, they have no degrees of comparison. Determiners are of a variety of types:

Articles are the adjectives *the*, *a* and *an*. *The* is called the *definite article* and indicates a particular, unique item. *A* and *an* are called *indefinite articles* and indicate a particular item from a number of similar items. *A* is used before a word that begins with a consonant sound; *an* is used before a word beginning with a vowel sound. Many people mistakenly think all words beginning with *h* take *an*, but only those with a silent *h* do. Others take *a*: **a** *historical play* (not **an** *historical play*).

The articles do not have comparative forms, and for that reason, some grammarians treat them as a separate part of speech. We'll go with the customary list of parts of speech and call them adjectives.

Demonstrative adjectives are ones that point to particular nouns or pronouns and agree in number with the words they modify. *That* and *this* are the singular demonstrative adjectives. *These* and *those* are the plural demonstrative adjectives.

Distributive adjectives include *each* and *every,* which are sometimes grouped with the demonstrative adjectives and called *pronominal adjectives* because all these words can also be used as pronouns rather than as modifiers.

Proper adjectives are proper nouns used as adjectives:

the *Soviet* people

Possessive adjectives are the same as what we've called possessive pronouns. Some linguists use this other label instead because they see possessives as always modifying a noun rather than taking its place.

Cardinal numbers (one, two, three) and ordinal numbers (first, second, third) are also used as determiners.

Nouns are often preceded by a whole cluster of determiners and other adjectives, sometimes with adverbs modifying the adjectives. These clusters are called *noun phrases*:

the first three happy years

his many less-obvious virtues

these several often-confused and misunderstood points

KINDS OF ADVERBS

You should become familiar with four kinds of adverbs, *simple adverbs, interrogative adverbs, conjunctive adverbs* and *sentence adverbs.*

Simple adverbs

Simple adverbs come before or after the word they modify:

He dressed *sloppily*. (modifies verb *dressed*)

the *sloppily* dressed man (modifies adjective *dressed*)

Frequently, writers mistakenly use an adjective when a simple adverb is required. We might see, for example, an ad asserting that a drink *goes down* **smooth**, when what's needed is the adverb *smoothly* to describe the manner in which it goes down. Or we might read a comparison that says one car *brakes* **quicker** than another, when, again, what's needed is an adverb, such as *more quickly*, to describe the manner in which the car brakes.

Interrogative adverbs

Interrogative adverbs ask a question:

Where are they? (modifies verb *are*)

Conjunctive adverbs

Conjunctive adverbs link a dependent clause to a previous clause or sentence:

His attorney said Fleming was considering his options *though* she thought a decision would be announced soon.

(See Chapter 4, page **61**.)

Sentence adverbs

Sentence adverbs may at first appear to be similar to conjunctive adverbs, but rather than linking a clause or sentence to another, they simply modify the sentence of which they are a part: *frankly, hopefully, personally, regrettably, sincerely, strictly speaking, to be honest*.

The most controversial sentence adverb is *hopefully*. Although most experts think it is ungrammatical to begin a sentence with *hopefully*, others, such as Geoffrey Nunberg and Jim Quinn, have defended it as a sentence adverb no better or no worse than any other.

One common objection to the use of the word is that it is not clear who is doing the hoping in a sentence like *Hopefully, it won't snow today.* Quinn, however, points out that Edwin Newman, an opponent of *hopefully*, uses another sentence adverb as the title of one of his books: "Strictly Speaking." Who's doing the strictly speaking, Quinn asks, in a sentence such as *Strictly speaking, you shouldn't use* **hopefully**? Obviously, the *speaker* is doing the strictly speaking or the hoping in such sentences, and nobody seems to be bothered by that with any sentence adverb other than *hopefully*.

Perhaps a better argument against *hopefully* used in this way is that the word means "in a hopeful manner." Obviously, a sentence such as *Hopefully, it won't snow today* doesn't mean *It won't snow today in a hopeful manner* but rather *I hope it won't snow today.* So, using *hopefully* this way results in not writing what is meant.

But language changes, and as words become more frequently used in certain ways, they often become more acceptable to language experts, who at some point decide they're fighting a losing cause. Already, The American Heritage Dictionary's usage panel has accepted in theory the use of *hopefully*, so we may eventually see more tolerance for this word in stylebooks. For now, however, because most editors and usage guides, including The AP Stylebook, object to using *hopefully* to mean "I hope" instead of "in a hopeful manner," we suggest you avoid it.

PARTICIPLES

We've already seen in Chapter 2 (page **33**) how participles (the forms of the verb usually ending in *-ing, -ed, -t* or *-en*) are used in making verb tenses and progressive forms.

The other major use for participles is as adjectives:

Talking, they reached an agreement. (*Talking* describes *they.*)

The frightened victim was *unhurt.* (*Frightened* and *unhurt* describe *victim.*)

Lawyers gathered *written* statements from the witnesses. (*Written* describes *statements.*)

And, though most books don't say so, participles are also used occasionally as prepositions, as in the cases of *regarding* and *excepting*.

The main problem with using participles as adjectives is misplacing them.

DANGLING PARTICIPLES AND OTHER MISPLACED MODIFIERS

A *participial phrase* (a group of related words beginning with a participle) should immediately precede the word it's modifying. When that doesn't happen, we have what's called a *dangling participle*—the participle is left dangling in front of the wrong word as though it modify that word instead of the one it should: *Marching down the street, he watched the parade.* In this example, the placement of the participial phrase suggests that the person watching the parade was marching down the street. Probably, however, he was standing still and the parade was moving. Note these further examples of dangling participles:

> Running down the street, his hat flew off. (Literally, that sentence says his hat was running down the street.)
>
> Taking our seats, the meeting began. (The meeting took our seats?)

Don't confuse a dangling participle with a *nominative absolute,* which is a noun or its substitute followed by participial phrase. A nominative absolute modifies the whole sentence rather than a noun or its substitute, so it acts as a sentence adverb:

> *The computer having gone down,* the paper was later. (*Computer* is a noun, having a participle.)
>
> The Tigers lost, *poor hitting being to blame.* (*Hitting* is a gerund, being a participle.)

Sometimes, the participial phrase is only implied:

> *The dog dead,* the boy cried inconsolably. (*Dog* is a noun. The participle *being* is implied between *dog* and *dead.*)

Unlike dangling participles, nominative absolutes are not considered ungrammatical, but if you have trouble distinguishing between the two, you should probably avoid both of them.

The dangling participle is the most frequent kind of **misplaced modifier**, or modifier in the wrong place at the wrong time. Changing the placement of a modifier in a sentence can change its meaning. If a modifier is put in the wrong place, the result can be either confusion or unintentional humor.

Journalist Jim Quinn cites this misplaced modifier: *Lincoln wrote the Gettysburg Address while riding on a train on the back of an envelope.* Because everyone would probably understand that the train was not on the back of the envelope, that sentence is more humorous than confusing.

Groucho Marx knowingly makes humorous use of a misplaced modifier in the movie "Animal Crackers" when he says: "*One morning, I shot an elephant in my pajamas. How he got in my pajamas I don't know.*" But most people who use misplaced modifiers don't intend to be funny.

Columnist James Kilpatrick has collected a number of misplaced modifiers that actually appeared in newspapers. The Anchorage Daily News, for example, carried a picture caption that said, "*Farmhand Bill Rud hoists a cow injured while giving birth to her feet with a front end loader while farm owner Tom Rogers looks on.*"

Here are a couple of examples Kilpatrick collected from The Associated Press:

In its coverage of the wedding of Sarah Ferguson and Prince Andrew, the wire service noted that "*Andrew, 26, is the son of Queen Elizabeth and a Royal Navy helicopter pilot.*" As Kilpatrick observes, "If so, the London press corps has missed one helluva story."

The wire service also reported about a man who was released after eight years in jail on a rape conviction: "*The case against Walker was dropped based on the results of a sperm sample taken from the victim's body, which had sat untested in the Elizabeth Police Department since the crime 12 years ago.*" Says Kilpatrick: "That body sat an awful long time."

The last example shows that misplaced modifiers don't just result in harmless laughs. Some readers would take offense that the careless writing unintentionally makes light of a serious situation. Others would be confused, as many would be reading the following sentence: *Facing an indictment on a tax-evasion charge, the City Council fired the public works director.* Who was facing an indictment? The City Council or the director?

The story is probably apocryphal, but it's said that the federal government once sent out a form to businesses asking how many employees they had broken down by sex. One confused manager replied, "We don't have anyone broken down by sex, but we do have a few alcoholics."

A less-spirited confusion can arise from the epithets newspaper reporters frequently attach to people's names as a way of working in additional information. For example, in a food-page story about how a man named Ken Kerry makes chili, the writer refers to *the lanky Texan, the former professor and the bearded editor* without clearly indicating that he means Kerry.

Sometimes the person's name *will* be repeated but with an age in front of it: *the 36-year-old Kerry.* This can look as though the reporter is trying to distinguish him from the 16-year-old Kerry or the 64-year-old Kerry. If such facts are vital, work them into sentences another way: *Kerry, 36, . . .*

ADVERB PLACEMENT

Adverbs, like adjectives, should be as close as possible to the word they modify. (Notice we didn't say **as close** *to the word they modify* **as possible**.) So, for example, instead of writing, *Bender* **just** *has* **one** *car*, write, *Bender has* **just one** *car*.

The word *only* poses a particular problem with placement, not only because it's frequently misplaced but also because writers are seldom aware of how confusing the result can be. Look at this sentence, for example: *Ostroushko only has one of the handmade instruments.* Does that mean he has *only one* or that *only Ostroushko* has one? The sentence should be rewritten to express more clearly whichever meaning was intended.

Some writers and editors mistakenly think that an adverb should never be placed in the middle of the parts of a compound-tense verb. For example, they would rewrite *The watch* **was consistently gaining** *time* as *The watch* **consistently was gaining** *time* or *The watch* **was gaining** *time* **consistently**.

But Wilson Follett, whose "Modern American Usage" is one of the most-quoted usage guides, says the placement of the adverb in such sentences should normally be between the two parts of the verb. He also offers this advice on alternative placements of adverbs:

- For emphasis, put the adverb at the start of the sentence:

Really, I don't want any.

- If the adverb is not needed for emphasis, put it in front of a single-word verb, between the helping verb and main verb, or after the first helping verb if there are more than one:

I *really want* some.

I *don't really want* any.

I *had really been wanting* some.

- If the adverb modifies the participle part of the verb alone, put it after the helping verbs:

Smoking **has been positively linked** *to higher rates of cancer.*

- If the adverb is a phrase, put it after the whole verb:

We *have heard again and again* the same thing from the city.

DOUBLE NEGATIVES

Avoid double negatives. Few of us would say *not never, not no, not none* or *not nothing,* but remember that the adverbs *hardly, rarely* and *scarcely* are also considered negative and do not take a *not.* So instead of saying He **can't hardly** *write,* say *He* **can hardly** *write.*

The word *but,* which is normally a conjunction, is also sometimes used as an adverb, and it, too, is considered negative. So instead of writing *She* **doesn't have but** *one friend,* write, *She* **has but** *one friend.* Instead of writing *I* **cannot help but** *sing,* write, *I* **cannot help** *singing.*

The prefixes *im-, in-, ir-, non-* and *un-* make adjectives negative, but negative adjectives may be used with negative adverbs: *It is* **not improbable** *that Gorbachev will go down in the history books as one of the greatest Soviet leaders.* Though such sentences are grammatically correct, it is usually clearer to write them more positively: *Gorbachev will probably go down in the history books as one of the greatest Soviet leaders.*

INTERJECTIONS

An interjection is an exclamation expressing strong emotion:

Ah!

Ouch!

Gee!

Not all grammarians consider interjections to be modifiers. In fact, many books say interjections don't have a grammatical connection to other words in a sentence.

Although often set off from the rest of the sentence by an exclamation mark, interjections also, however, are frequently connected to the beginning of the sentence by a comma. Written this way—which is common because journalists don't like to use exclamation points—they work as sentence adverbs, modifying the entire sentence. Grammarians who consider them adverbs rather than a separate part of speech note that interjections don't have the comparative forms of other adverbs.

In general, the interjection is the part of speech that gives the least trouble. But a couple of rules are worth noting:

- Never put more than one exclamation point behind an interjection (or anywhere else for that matter).

- Avoid profanity in family publications such as newspapers, unless, as The AP Stylebook says, the words "are part of direct quotations, and there is a compelling reason for them."

CHAPTER 4

Connecting Words: Prepositions, Conjunctions, Conjunctive Adverbs and Relative Pronouns

Prepositions, conjunctions, conjunctive adverbs and *relative pronouns* are words used to connect other words or groups of words. *Prepositions* connect nouns or their substitutes to another word or other words in the sentence. *Conjunctions* connect words, phrases or clauses. *Conjunctive adverbs* are used like conjunctions, but conjunctive adverbs also show a logical relationship between the words, phrases or clauses they connect in a way that conjunctions do not. *Relative pronouns* are used to introduce dependent clauses that modify a noun or pronoun—clauses that are sometimes called *relative clauses*.

PREPOSITIONS

Prepositions show the relationship between the noun or noun substitute following them and something else in the sentence. The preposition, the noun or noun substitute following it (the *object of the preposition)* and any words modifying the object form a *prepositional phrase.* Prepositional phrases usually act as either adjectives or adverbs:

The computer *with two disk drives* is more expensive. (works as an adjective modifying *computer)*

The suspect was seen running *from the scene of the crime.* (works as an adverb modifying *running)*

Prepositions usually indicate direction (*to, toward, over, under, from*) or location (*on, at, beside, near*).
Here's an easy way to spot most of these types of prepositions:

Imagine a bird and some trees. Prepositions are those words that describe the relationship the bird could have with the trees as it flies. It could fly *between* the trees, *toward* the trees, *in* the trees, *at* the trees, *from* the trees, *under* the trees, *over* the trees, *for* the trees and so on.

In addition to these two most common types of prepositions, some show time (*in, at, during, until*); some indicate possession (*of, with*); some show responsibility (*for*) or agency (*by*); some exclude (*except, without*); and some show similarity (*like*).

In form, prepositions may be single words (*at, to, from*), compound words (*into, upon*) or phrases (*according to, because of, in accordance with, in spite of* and *on top of*). Sometimes, participles are used as prepositions (*excepting, regarding*).

USES AND MISUSES OF PREPOSITIONS

At the end of a sentence

The best-known of rules about prepositions is not to end a sentence with one. Our guess is that this rule goes back to the 18th-century English grammar books that based their rules on Latin grammar rather than on how the English language actually works. Because Latin words have different endings depending on the role they play in a sentence, words in Latin sentences can be moved around, but the sentence will still mean the same thing. The exception is the rule that a Latin sentence cannot end with a preposition.

Almost as famous as the rule, however, is Winston Churchill's rejoinder beloved by all who hate learning silly rules: *"This is the sort of English up with which I will not put."* The fact is, English speakers have ended sentences with prepositions for hundreds of years, and some sentences, such as Churchill's, sound awkward when they don't end with a preposition. For example: *What are you waiting for?* It just doesn't sound good to turn it around: *For what are you waiting?*

Still, it's a good idea to avoid the wrath of your editor and to try to rewrite a sentence that ends with a preposition. This is usually easy, though some sentences require more effort. For example, *They're fun to add your own touches to* may be a puzzler at first, but some thought might yield *It's fun to add your own touches to them.*

57

Parallel prepositions

Some editors insist that parallel prepositional phrases repeat the preposition. For example: *The protesters said they were concerned **about** pollution and **about** road congestion.* We, however, wouldn't insist on the second *about* in a sentence that is clear without it—as that one would be.

Sometimes, though, parallel prepositions help avoid confusion: *The protesters said they were concerned about pollution from the plant and about road congestion.* Drop the second *about* in that sentence, and it isn't clear whether the protesters are concerned about pollution *and* road congestion or about pollution that comes from the plant and *from* road congestion.

Here's another example of a sentence that is confusing for lack of a parallel preposition: *Obscurantism means opposition to progress or enlightenment.* Does this mean obscurantism *is* enlightenment or opposition *to* it? If the former, reverse the sentence order: *Obscurantism means enlightenment or opposition to progress.* If it's the latter, add *to* before enlightenment: *Obscurantism means opposition to progress or to enlightenment.* (By the way, it's the latter.)

Separating proper nouns

Prepositions can be helpful in separating items that might otherwise run together confusingly. Usually, this involves proper nouns next to each other: *Ted Winston Sunday said . . .* In such cases, either put *on* between *Winston* and *Sunday,* or rewrite: *Ted Winston said Sunday . . .*

Prepositions as part of the verb

Most copy editors have been taught not to break a multiple-line headline in the middle of a prepositional phrase, but an exception should be made for a preposition that is part of the verb. Except in a one-column headline, it is not normally acceptable to end a line of a headline with a preposition and to have its object on the next line. But some prepositions are actually a part of the verb rather than part of a prepositional phrase. We don't just mean the *to* in an infinitive. Sometimes, a preposition *after* a verb is part of that verb. You can spot such instances by asking whether leaving off the preposition changes the meaning of the verb. Here are some:

carry out	head off	look up to
come about	look after	pick up
come by	look for	put on
come into	look in on	take off
come through	look into	think up
come to	look on	try out
come upon	look up	work out

It is probably advisable to end a line of a headline with such a verb-preposition combination, rather than moving the preposition to the next line, because here the preposition makes more sense grouped with the verb.

CONJUNCTIONS

A conjunction connects words, phrases or clauses. It's easier to see what's meant by looking at a few examples of conjunctions: *and, because, but, either . . . or, neither . . . nor, or, so that* and *yet.*.

Coordinating (coordinate) conjunctions

Coordinating conjunctions—such as *and, but, for, nor, or* and *yet*—are used when the words, phrases or clauses they connect are of equal rank. How do we know when they're of equal rank? The rule is that a word equals another word (*wine* **and** *roses*); a phrase equals another phrase (*to be* **or** *not to be*); an independent clause equals an independent clause (*I'm going,* **and** *I'm not coming back*); and a dependent clause equals another dependent clause (*He said school desegregation would follow if the court rules in the group's favor* **or** *if the group wins enough seats on the board*).

If a coordinating conjunction is used to connect two independent clauses, put a comma before the conjunction:

The judge said he would open the hearing to the press, but he didn't.

This old rule has been loosened somewhat in recent years, and it is now permissible to begin a sentence with a coordinating conjunction—most frequently *but*. So, for emphasis, you could write: *The judge said he would open the hearing to the press. But he didn't.* (For more on clauses, see Chapter 5, page **64**.)

Correlative conjunctions

Correlative conjunctions are similar to coordinating conjunctions in that they connect words, phrases or clauses of equal rank. The difference is that correlative conjunctions are used in pairs:

as . . . as	neither . . . nor
as well . . . as	not only . . . but also
both . . . and	not so . . . as
either . . . or ·	since . . . therefore
if . . . then	whether . . . or

Most writers have long since mastered the fact that *either* and *or* go together, as do *neither* and *nor*—though editors occasionally find spots where someone has mistakenly written *neither . . . or*. Not many journalists, however, seem to know that *not only . . .* must always be followed by *but also* or that the negative form of *as . . . as* is *not so . . . as*:

Not only blacks but also many whites voted for Jackson in the South.

Note that sometimes the *but* is replaced by a colon or semi-colon:

Not only blacks voted for Jackson in the South: Many whites did, also.)

It is *as* long *as* it is wide.

It is *not so* long *as* it is wide.

Subordinating (subordinate) conjunctions

Subordinating conjunctions—such as *although, as, because, if, since, though, until, whether* and *while*—connect two unequal parts of a sentence. Most often, these unequal parts are independent and dependent clauses. Subordinating conjunctions typically introduce dependent clauses that modify the independent clause by explaining cause, contrast, reason or time. (See Chapter 5, page **65**.)

Generally speaking, you don't need a comma before subordinating conjunctions because they introduce dependent clauses. The main dispute is over *because*. Some books say a clause introduced by *because* is always preceded by a comma, but journalists usually only put a comma before a conjunction if it introduces an independent clause—so never put one before *because*. (For more on punctuation, see Chapter 6, page **79**.)

CONJUNCTIVE ADVERBS

Conjunctive adverbs are good transition words because, in connecting sentences, they act as adverbs by showing a logical relationship. To see this distinction, compare the conjunctive adverbs listed below with the conjunctions on page **60**:

accordingly	hence	most important
also	henceforth	namely
anyhow	however	nevertheless
at the same time	in addition	on the contrary
besides	indeed	on the other hand
consequently	instead	otherwise
first	in the first place	second
for example	likewise	still
for this reason	meanwhile	therefore
furthermore	moreover	thus

Unlike conjunctions, which always come at the beginning of the clauses they introduce, conjunctive adverbs often can be placed at the beginning, in the middle or at the end of a clause. Writing adviser William Zinsser, in fact, believes that although *however* can be placed in any of those positions, it works best in the middle of the clause. Another way conjunctive adverbs differ from conjunctions is that, unlike conjunctions, conjunctive adverbs may be used at the beginning of a clause after a semicolon: *The battle was over;* **however,** *all was not still.* Journalists generally avoid this use, however, because they prefer, as a rule, not to use semicolons.

RELATIVE PRONOUNS

Relative pronouns (*who, whom, whose, which, that* and sometimes *what*) are pronouns that introduce dependent clauses closely connected with the relative pronoun's antecedent. Such dependent clauses are called *relative clauses*. While working as connectives, relative pronouns also serve as the subject or object of the clause in which they occur.

The choice of the correct relative pronoun depends on three things: the antecedent, restrictiveness and case.

The antecedent

When the antecedent is a collective noun (such as the name of an association, business or governing body), a thing (inanimate object, abstraction and so on) or an animal without a proper-noun name, the correct relative pronoun is *which, that* or *what*. When the antecedent is a person or an animal with a name, the correct relative pronoun is *who, whom* or *whose*:

Mobil is the oil company *that* (not *who*) wants to invite you to support public television. (collective noun)

Which is the dog that bit the child? (animal without a name)

What is the color of that scarf? (thing)

Who is this playwright Horner *whom* everyone is discussing? (person)

This is Fluffy, *who* just had kittens. (animal with a name)

Restrictiveness

Choosing between *that* and *which* depends on whether the relative clause is essential to (restricts the meaning of) the sentence in which it appears. *Which* sets off something non-restrictive (non-essential), *that* something restrictive (essential). (For a detailed discussion of restrictiveness, with specific examples using *that* and *which*, see Chapter 5, page **66**.)

Case

Choosing among *who* (nominative), *whom* (objective) and *whose* (possessive) depends on case. (See Chapter 1, page **14**.)

Phrases, Clauses and Sentences

A *phrase* is a group of related words that lacks either a subject or a predicate, or both. A *clause* is a group of related words with a subject and a predicate. A *sentence*, like a clause, also is a group of related words with a subject and predicate, but in addition it must make a complete statement. That last requirement has never been defined to our satisfaction, although native speakers of English seem to be able to recognize most sentences when they see them.

PHRASES

Just as single words may be substantives (nouns or their substitutes), verbs, modifiers or connectives, so can phrases.

Phrases as substantives:

Playing the mandolin is like *plucking a violin*. (two gerund phrases, the first used as the subject of the sentence, the second the object of the preposition like)

To try is *to succeed*. (two infinitive phrases, the first the subject of the sentence, the second the predicate nominative)

Over there is where police found the body. (prepositional phrase used as the subject of the sentence)

Phrases as verbs:

Wagner *had been going* to college for three years at the time. (main verb *going* with two helping verbs)

I *ought not eat* this, but it's too good to pass up. (main verb eat with helping verb *ought* and adverb *not*)

Phrases as modifiers:

Looking through the book, Miller decided to buy it. (participial phrase used as an adjective modifying *Miller*)

Benitez had long been wanting to go *to the Caribbean*. (prepositional phrase used as an adverb modifying the infinitive *to go*)

Phrases as connectives:

In spite of that, the commission turned down the request. (phrasal preposition takes place of a single one such as *despite*)

The programs are *similar to* each other. (phrasal preposition takes place of a single one such as *like*)

CLAUSES

Independent clauses

An *independent (or main) clause* is one that can stand alone as a complete sentence. You may think of it as a sentence within a sentence; other clauses often will be attached to it to make a longer sentence. In a sentence with more than one independent clause, one of the clauses may start with a coordinating conjunction or a conjunctive adverb:

Here we are.

Here we are, *and here we go again.*

Here we are; *moreover, here we go again.*

Dependent clauses

A *dependent clause* is one that cannot stand alone as a complete sentence but must be joined to an independent clause. That's because dependent clauses work as nouns, adjectives or adverbs rather than as complete statements.

Examples of independent and dependent clauses are in this sentence from Ernest Hemingway's "A Moveable Feast":

If you are lucky enough to have lived in Paris as a young man, then wherever you go for the rest of your life, it stays with you, for Paris is a moveable feast. (*It stays with you* is the independent clause; the others are all dependent.)

There are two kinds of dependent clauses:

***Subordinate clauses* begin with a *subordinating conjunction* (Chapter 4, page 60):**

The City Council rejected the idea *because no one really pushed for it.* (subordinate clause acting as an adverb modifying rejected)

***Relative clauses* begin with a *relative pronoun* (see Chapter 4, page 61):**

Whoever made that rule no longer works here. (relative clause working in place of a noun as the subject)

He never did figure out *who had been at the door.* (relative clause acting in place of a noun as the direct object)

The person *who was here* left. (relative clause acting as an adjective modifying person)

USES AND MISUSES OF PHRASES AND CLAUSES

Restrictive vs. non-restrictive elements

Phrases and clauses (and sometimes even single words) can be classified as either *restrictive (essential)* or *non-restrictive (non-essential).* A restrictive phrase or clause is essential to a sentence's meaning and is not set off by commas. A non-restrictive phrase or clause is not essential to a sentence's meaning and is set off by commas, dashes or parentheses. Journalists tend to avoid parentheses, and use commas or dashes, depending on the length of pause they want.

An easy way to distinguish a restrictive from a non-restrictive element is to ask yourself whether it could be set off in parentheses. If it could, then it's non-restrictive, so set it off with commas.

Here are some examples of words, phrases and clauses that are non-restrictive (non-essential) and should be set off with commas:

"Yes, *Juanita,* I'm over here." (*Juanita* is a noun of direct address and is non-essential—the sentence means the same thing without it).

Dwight, *my jazz-musician friend,* just cut an album. (The phrase *my jazz-musician friend* is acting as an appositive and is non-essential.)

65

"Beautiful Losers," *a novel by Canadian poet Leonard Cohen,* combines spirituality and sexuality. (The phrase *a novel by Canadian poet Leonard Cohen* works as an adjective modifying "Beautiful Losers" and is non-essential.)

That actor—*who had never played professionally before*—won the part. (The relative clause *who had never played professionally before* works as an adjective modifying actor.)

Knowing the difference between restrictive and non-restrictive elements often makes a difference in understanding the meaning of a sentence. Take a look at this sentence, for example: *Their daughter Dawn visited with her husband, Kirk.* The lack of commas around *Dawn* indicates they have more than one daughter, so the name is essential to the meaning of the sentence. *Kirk,* however, is set off by a comma, which indicates Dawn has only one husband, so his name is not essential to the meaning of the sentence.

Compare these non-restrictive and restrictive versions of similar sentences:

When he was a child, he said, other boys made fun of him. (The commas around *he said* indicate that those two words are not essential. They simply tell us that a statement was made later in life about incidents that happened during childhood.)

When he was a child, he said other boys made fun of him. (Here, a comma sets off only the introductory clause. The lack of a comma after he said indicates those two words are essential to the independent clause. In other words, he made the statement when he was a child rather than later in life.)

That vs. which

Confusion about when to use clauses introduced by *that* and *which* is common among writers. *Which* is the one to use when what is introduced is not essential to the meaning of the sentence. Clauses introduced by the word *which* usually must be set off with commas.

The Nile is the river *that* gives Egypt life. (restrictive)

The Nile, *which* flows into the Mediterranean, gives Egypt life. (non-restrictive)

If you think of a non-essential clause as an aside, then you can remember that *which* introduces a clause set off by parentheses, dashes or commas. *That* introduces an essential clause not set off with parentheses, dashes or commas. Examples:

The lawn mower *that* is broken (essential because tells which one) is in the garage.

The lawn mower, *which* is broken (non-essential because merely adds a fact parenthetically about the only lawn mower), is in the garage.

The corner house, *which has a brick front*, was ours. (non-essential)

The house *that has a brick front* is ours. (essential)

SENTENCES

On the simplest level, a *sentence* consists of a subject and a predicate—that is, someone or something doing or being: "*Existence exists*," says Ayn Rand in a grammatically simple but philosophically complex sentence. In some sentences, the subject is understood, as in a command: *Run!* Sometimes the sentence will contain a direct object and sometimes an indirect object: *The president sent Congress the bill.* Sometimes the sentence will contain a predicate complement: "*This looks like the big one*," the general said. Sentences also may contain modifiers and additional phrases and clauses.

Sentences classified by function

Sentences can be classified according to four functions:

A *declarative sentence* makes a statement of fact:

Baseball is our national sport.

An *interrogative sentence* asks a question:

What is our national sport?

An *exclamatory sentence* expresses surprise or emotion:

What a great day for baseball!

An *imperative sentence* expresses a command or request:

Play ball!

Sentences classified by form

Mastering the forms of sentences will give your writing variety:

A *simple sentence* has one independent clause:

The team is in a slump.

Note that a sentence may have more than one subject and verb and still be a simple sentence because it has just one independent clause:

The team and the coach are hoping and praying. (has a compound subject and compound predicate but only one clause)

A *compound sentence* has two or more independent clauses connected by a comma and a coordinating conjunction (*and, but, for, or, nor, yet*), a conjunctive adverb (*accordingly, also, anyhow, besides, consequently, however, moreover, nevertheless, otherwise, still, then, therefore, thus, yet*), a semicolon, or a conjunctive adverb and a semicolon:

The team is in a slump, but the coach is concerned.

The team is in a slump, though the coach is unconcerned.

The team is in a slump; the coach is concerned.

The team is in a slump; however, the coach is unconcerned.

Compound sentences are used to show that thoughts are related and equal.

A *complex sentence* contains one independent clause and one or more dependent clauses:

The team was in a slump already when its best pitcher broke his arm.

Dependent clauses are subordinated to the independent clause by subordinate conjunctions (*as, as if, as though, because, before, if, since, that, till, unless, when, where, whether*) or relative pronouns (*that, that which, what, which, who, whom, whose*). If you see subordinate conjunctions or relative pronouns, then what follows is probably a dependent clause.

One bit of advice about complex sentences: It's usually clearer not to separate the subject and verb of an independent clause with a dependent clause. *The president, though the Cabinet advised against it, vetoed the measure* would read better as *The president vetoed the measure though the Cabinet advised against it.*

A *compound-complex sentence* contains two or more independent clauses and one or more dependent clauses:

The cat was on the mat, and the dog was eyeing him when I came home.

Compound-complex sentences usually are too long to make good leads for articles, so if you've led with one, consider breaking it down.

Sentences classified by style

There are three kinds of sentences according to their style:

A *periodic sentence* has the main thought at the end, so it's usually a dependent clause followed by an independent one:

When you want to emphasize, use periodic sentences.

Periodic sentences imitate the way the mind works—rambling a bit, before coming to the point. They work well in writing—if they're not overused—because the main point is the final impression in the reader's mind. In conversation, however, they can label you a bore.

A *loose sentence* has the main thought at the front, so it's usually an independent clause followed by a dependent clause or other modification:

Use loose sentences to state the idea early, before you provide qualifications and additions.

A *balanced sentence* has two parts of equal importance that are set up in balance or contrast, so it's usually two independent clauses:

Periodic sentences often work better in print; loose sentences tend to work better in conversation.

COMMON SENTENCE PROBLEMS

The philosopher Eric Hoffer said, "There are few things so subtle and beautiful as a good sentence." Unfortunately, many sentences fall short. Here are some common ways they go astray:

Fragments

A *fragment* is a word or group of words that isn't a complete sentence. Either it lacks a subject or predicate, or it's a dependent clause:

A team for all seasons.

Takes the guesswork out of the game.

Because he was sick.

Fragments are becoming acceptable to more editors these days, but they should not be used unless you have a specific reason. For example, fiction writers use them to capture the way people speak. Ad writers use them to emphasize a product name: "*Bertha's Kitty Boutique. For people who care about cats.*" And some grammarians are now willing to accept them under certain circumstances.

For example, some consider an answer to a question a complete sentence even though it may be incomplete on the surface—they consider the other elements implied: *Why didn't he come? **Because he was sick***. Some are also willing to accept a brief transition or a short question as a sentence:

And now the news.

Why?

What more could I do? Sing? Dance?

Sometimes acceptable fragments are called *condensed sentences* because, unlike unacceptable fragments, they represent—in a condensed statement—a full sentence.

Fused sentences

Fused sentences unacceptably combine two or more sentences without punctuation between them.

The boy went to town the girl did, too.

Fused sentences would only be acceptable in non-fiction as a quotation from the writings of a semiliterate person.

Comma-splice sentences

Comma-splice sentences **unacceptably connect two or more independent clauses with only a comma**:

They are going, we are going also.

Although journalists should normally avoid comma-splice sentences, some writers, such as Kurt Vonnegut, use comma-splices occasionally to imitate conversation. Also, many grammarians now say that a series of short sentences may be connected with commas, if you like, as in Caesar's famous "*I came, I saw, I conquered.*" (It could also be translated with semicolons or periods.)

Run-on sentences

Run-on sentences **may or may not be grammatical, but they make little sense because unrelated items, unimportant details or extra clauses were added as though the writer didn't know when to stop**.

Hemingway sometimes uses this device to cover ground quickly and let the gaps imply things he doesn't want to spell out. It can be a way of avoiding sentimentality by understating. The following run-on sentence, though not Hemingway, is either acceptable or not depending on how effective you judge it:

The blind man's seeing-eye dog died, and it was a sad occasion, and all the man's friends went to the funeral then went to the bar and drank to his health and said how unfair it was.

Such a sentence might work in fiction, but no newspaper editor would approve it.

William Faulkner to the contrary, the best sentences rarely are longer than 2½ typed lines. Sentences containing much technical information shouldn't average more than about 20 words.

Lack of parallelism

When parallel ideas are not expressed in a parallel manner, the rhythm of the sentence is thrown off and the logical relationships are made less clear. How do you make ideas parallel? In a series, all the items should be alike, whether all nouns, all gerunds, all infinitives, all phrases or all clauses. If a series of verbs is used, they should all be in the same tense, voice and mood. Subjects of parallel clauses should be in the same person and number. When two phrasal prepositions or conjunctions are used together, both need to be present in their entirety.

Here are some examples, first of sentences lacking parallel structure, then of the same sentences rewritten correctly.

Wrong: He admires Kathy for her intelligence, energy and because she is a good leader. (nouns and clause not balanced)

Right: He admires Kathy for her intelligence, energy and leadership.

Wrong: First, he walked in, then he smiled, then he says, "Hello." (past and present tenses mixed)

Right: First, he walked in, then he smiled, then he said, "Hello."

Wrong: He enjoyed gathering information and then to write about it. (gerund and infinitive not balanced)

Right: He enjoyed gathering information and then writing about it.

Wrong: She was presented the award then left. (passive and active voice in same sentence)

Right: She accepted the award then left.

Wrong: The teacher was both informed, and she cared about her students. (participle and clause not balanced; active and passive voice mixed)

Right: The teacher was both informed about the subject and caring toward her students.

Wrong: One should be prepared; you never know who might call. (person of subjects not balanced)

Right: One should be prepared; one never knows who might call.

Wrong: The fishing equipment cost as much or more than a bicycle. (conjunctions not balanced because part of one missing)

Right: The fishing equipment cost as much as or more than a bicycle.

SUBJECT-VERB AGREEMENT

Subject-verb agreement problems are some of the most common ways sentences go wrong. A singular subject needs a singular verb, and a plural subject needs a plural verb. Although that sounds easy enough, there are a number of tricky situations that confuse writers.

Subject and predicate nominative in disagreement

When the subject is plural and the predicate nominative singular or vice versa, many people are unsure what the number of the verb should be. The answer is easy. The number of the verb should always agree with the number of the subject. Both of the following sentences, therefore, are correct:

The committee *is* Ernie Havens, Ruth Brent and Bree Oliver.

Ernie Havens, Ruth Brent and Bree Oliver *are* the committee.

Nouns or pronouns between the subject and verb

If a noun or pronoun comes between the subject and verb, the verb still agrees with the subject, not this other noun or pronoun:

Wednesday's newspaper, along with its supplements, is our biggest edition ever. (The subject is the singular noun newspaper. The phrase along with its supplements is a parenthetical modifier, so the plural noun supplements does not influence the number of the verb.)

No one but they knows the location. (The subject is no one. They does not influence the verb because it is not the subject.)

Subjects following verbs

Although the subject precedes the verb in most sentences, sometimes the subject follows the verb and can cause subject-verb agreement problems. Questions, the most common place where this occurs, usually don't cause much confusion, but here are a couple of other situations in which this problem arises:

In a sentence beginning with *here* or *there*, the verb agrees with the number of the subject, which follows the verb:

> Here *comes* the cake.
>
> Here *come* the bicyclists.
>
> Here *come* the horse and rider.

Especially a problem is the verb *to be* after *here* or *there*. Many people always seem to turn the combination into a contraction with a singular verb:

> Here *are* (not *Here's*) the papers I promised you.
>
> There *are* (not *There's*) no two ways about it.

Stilted sentences sometimes invert the sentence order: *Out of the room stomps the student*. Rewriting such sentences in normal order not only sounds better but also makes it less likely that the verb will be assigned the wrong number: *The student stomps out of the room*.

Collective nouns vs. uncountable nouns

Collective nouns are singular in form but plural in meaning. When it comes to verb agreement, form triumphs over function, and they generally take singular verbs.

The collective nouns include: *army, assembly, audience, board, breed, cast, choir, class, club, commission, committee, community, company, corporation, council, couple, covey, crew, crowd, department, faculty, family, firm, flock, furniture, gang, group, herd, jury, mob, orchestra, panel, press, public, remainder, staff, team, union and United States*. The names of associations, boards, companies and so on are also considered collective nouns.

As we said, the verb after a collective noun is usually singular. The rule is this:

Use the singular form when the noun is being used in the sense of a single group operating together in agreement; use the plural form if the noun is used to name a group operating as individuals or in disagreement.

The jury *was* unanimous. But The jury *were* split. (Sounds odd, but you can't always trust your ear when it comes to traditional grammar. To avoid the obvious ugliness of The jury were split, it is possible to add the word members after jury, or, better yet, to substitute the word jurors.)

Uncountable (also called non-countable) nouns are ones that have no plural though many of them look plural already. They are not so consistent as collective nouns in that some take a singular verb, some a plural.

These uncountables take a singular verb: *advice, apparatus, athletics, civics, courage, economics, fun, health, information, jazz, linguistics, mathematics, measles, mumps, news, remainder, shambles, summons* and *whereabouts.*

These uncountables take a plural verb: *assets, barracks, earnings, goods, kudos, odds, pants, pliers, proceeds, remains, riches, scissors, shears, tactics, thanks, tongs* and *wages.*

These uncountables may take singular or plural depending on context: *ethics, gross, headquarters, mechanics, politics, savings, series, species* and *statistics.* Example: *Politics is her favorite subject.* But *Her politics are socialistic.*

Other problems with nouns

- Don't mistake plural nouns ending in *-a* with their singular forms ending in *-um. Criteria, data* and *media* are plural, not singular. (For more examples, see Chapter 1, pages **12–13**.)

- Units of measurement, such as distances, money, time and weight, sometimes take a singular verb even though they themselves are plural in form. This happens when the amount can be seen as a single amount: *Five dollars* **is** *not too much to ask of a friend.*

- *Couple, majority, number* and *total* are singular if preceded by *the*, plural if preceded by *a.*

  The number of people expected *is* small.

  A number of people *are* expected to attend.

- Fractions and percentages are singular or plural depending on the noun or pronoun following them:

  One-third of the *book is* a flashback.

  One-third of the *customers are* regulars.

Fifty percent of the *budget is* for debt retirement.

Fifty percent of the *cases are* cured.

Indefinite pronouns

Indefinite pronouns confuse many writers. *Both, few, many, others* and *several* are plural. *Another, anybody, anyone, anything, each one, either, everybody, everyone, everything, little, many a, more than one, much, neither, nobody, no one, nothing, other, somebody, someone* and *something* are singular, even though some of them seem to refer to more than one. *All, any, each, more, most, none, plenty, some* and *such* can be either singular or plural depending on the context:

All are here. But *All is* lost.

Some are coming. But *Some is* left.

Some of the indefinite pronouns are worth a special look:

- Despite the pleas of most authorities (including Theodore Bernstein, Bergen Evans, William and Mary Morris and The American Heritage Dictionary) that *none* is more often plural than singular, most people are taught to make it singular all the time—and they will think you have made a mistake if you make it plural. The AP Stylebook's rule is a compromise that recognizes *none* can be plural but that makes it singular in most instances. AP style makes *none* singular if it means no single one (which it means most of the time), or plural if the sense is no two or no amount:

  None of the people invited *has* arrived. (not one)

  None of the experts *agree*. (no two)

- *Each* is singular if it comes before the verb, plural if after: **Each is** *going by car*. But *They* **are each** *going by car*. (Don't write *They* **each are** going by car.)

- *Either* and *neither* used by themselves are singular pronouns. For example, *Neither of them* **have** *come* should be rewritten as *Neither of them* **has** *come*. *Either of the two* **work** *hard* should be rewritten as *Either of the two* **works** *hard*.

    But in the constructions *either . . . or* or *neither . . . nor*, the words are used as conjunctions, not pronouns. The verb following them is singular or plural depending on whether the noun or pronoun following *or* or *nor* is singular or plural. For example, these two sentences both are correct:

Neither John nor Bill *is* going.

Neither John nor his parents *are* going.

Relative pronouns

A verb following a relative pronoun (*that, which, who, whom*) has the same person and number as the pronoun's antecedent:

We who *are* gone salute you.

An apparent exception to the rule about a pronoun agreeing in number with its antecedent is the word *what* used as a relative pronoun. When used as a subject, *what* takes a singular verb even if its complement is plural. For example, "*Votes are what count in elections*" is wrong; it should be "*Votes are what counts in elections.*" That's because *what*, the subject of the dependent clause *what counts in elections*, is synonymous with *that which*, and so is singular. (The subject of the independent clause, *votes*, is plural and takes a plural verb, *are*.)

Prepositional phrases

If a subject contains a prepositional phrase, remember that in almost all instances the noun or pronoun following the preposition is not the actual subject, so the verb instead agrees with the substantive before the preposition:

Only one of the professors *seems* to care.

An exception occurs after a phrase beginning with *one of (the, those, these)* and ending with *who, which* or *that*. Here, the real subject of the dependent clause is the noun or pronoun following *of*:

She is one of those people who *are* always on time. (Of the people who are always on time, she is one.)

He thinks he is one of those people who *are* never wrong. (Of the people who are never wrong, he thinks he is one.)

But if the *one* in such a construction is preceded by *only*, the *one* is considered the antecedent, and the construction becomes singular again:

She is the only one of those people who *is* always on time.

He thinks he is the only one of those people who *is* never wrong.

Conjunctions

***And* connecting two or more items in a subject usually makes it plural**:

Joe and Dan *are* coming to the party.

The exception is when the words connected by *and* are part of a single thing:

Pork and beans *is* not my favorite dish.

***Or* used alone to connect two or more items in a subject makes the verb singular unless one of the items in the subject is plural. Then, the verb agrees with the nearest noun or pronoun**:

Mary Teagate or Phil Anderson *is* answering calls today.

Mary Teagate or they *are* answering calls today.

The number of the subject is not affected by phrases beginning with words that are set off with commas—such as *along with, as well as, in addition to, including, such as* or *together with*:

John, as well as they, *is* going.

When the correlative conjunction *not only . . . but also* is used, there should not be a comma before the *but also*, and the verb, therefore, should be plural.

CHAPTER 6

Punctuation

Punctuation is one of the least agreed-upon parts of writing, despite the fact that it's been around longer than traditional grammar. (English punctuation grew out of Gregorian chant notations, but traditional English grammar wasn't codified until the 18th century.) Grammar books often disagree about punctuation, and stylebooks get in the act and disagree some more.

Luckily, most journalists accept The AP Stylebook as an arbiter of punctuation. But sometimes, learning the stylebook's rules is one thing and applying them is something else. We've found that a knowledge of phrases, clauses and sentence structure is the key to correct punctuation. It helps you remember the rules, understand them and figure out solutions when the rules in the stylebook don't go far enough.

PERIODS, EXCLAMATION POINTS AND QUESTION MARKS

If only all punctuation were as easy as using these three symbols!

Periods, exclamation points and question marks don't give writers much trouble, so we won't go into all their uses. Instead, we'll just note the few problems with them that show up frequently.

It's been said that the main problem journalists have with periods is not using enough of them. Writers sometimes let sentences run too long, shoehorning too many ideas into too little space.

Sometimes, too, journalists have trouble knowing when to use periods in abbreviations, a subject we cover in our summary of the rules of abbreviation. (See Appendix B, page **218**.)

One other quick note about periods: With computers, leave just one space behind a period instead of the two that are left with a typewriter. The typesetting equipment will do a better job spacing this way.

Journalists generally confine the use of exclamation points to quotations in which people express strong emotion or to opinions expressed in editorials or personal columns. In other uses, exclamation marks run the risk of making an article sound biased, sensational or gushy. Still, they have their place, as in the first sentence of this section.

Occasionally, someone will double the exclamation points to show extra emphasis or combine an exclamation point with a question mark to indicate a question asked emotionally. Don't do either of these things. Exclamation points and question marks are terminal punctuation marks that signal a full stop—so only one is needed.

As for question marks, don't use one after an indirect quotation. Rewrite *He said he wondered how it got there?* as *He said he wondered how it got there.*

Also, journalists should avoid putting a question mark in parentheses to suggest dubiousness: *The music (?) consisted of squawks and static.* Such a practice has no place in a news story, which readers expect to be as free as possible of personal opinion.

COMMAS

Knowing when to use commas is probably the most difficult part of learning to punctuate properly. Many people just put commas wherever they want a pause. This works to an extent but not completely.

Here are some rules for comma placement that incorporate but go beyond those in The AP Stylebook. They'll provide consistency in situations the stylebook doesn't cover.

Always use a comma

First, here are instances in which you should *always* use commas:

1. Use a comma after *said* when introducing a direct quotation one sentence long:

Cooper said, ''To leave out premarital testing from this bill is like taking a Missouri census and leaving out Kansas City.''

80

2. Use a comma before and after the abbreviation for a state following a city, and before and after a year following a month and date. This rule may be contrary to what you learned in English classes, but it is the way journalists do it:

Roberto and Carmen met in Pulaski, Tenn., at the Butter Bowl.

On May 2, 1987, the two giants in the field met.

3. Use a comma after words in a series but not before the conjunction unless the meaning would be unclear:

The new budget proposals would cut spending for student loans, building repairs, road improvements and farm subsidies.

What would be an example of a series that would be unclear without a comma before the conjunction? One in which the same conjunction appears earlier in the series as part of an item:

He went to town to buy a can of corn, a can of peas and carrots, and a can of beans.

_Do_ use a comma before the word _etc._ at the end of a series:

Send us what you've got: the books, the tapes, etc.

4. Use a comma after introductory clauses, phrases or words:

The House approved the measure, and so did the Senate. (The comma follows an introductory independent clause in a compound sentence.)

Because his mother insisted, he gave college a second chance. (The comma follows an introductory dependent clause in a complex sentence.)

Listening to the band, he decided to audition. (The comma follows an introductory participial phrase.)

In July, Taylor was born. (The comma follows an introductory prepositional phrase.)

Often, she was without shelter. (Most writers and editors are inconsistent about commas after introductory adverbs such as this one. Sometimes, they put them in; sometimes, they don't, depending on whether they would pause there when saying the sentence. But such a subjective approach wastes time and money because a writer may put in a comma that an editor will take out and a proofreader put back. We suggest always putting a comma after all introductory words, phrases or clauses, even when they're only one word long.)

Gee, that smells good. (The comma follows an introductory interjection. For added emphasis, you could use an exclamation point either after the interjection or after good. If after the interjection, we would capitalize *that*.)

5. Use a comma between two independent clauses joined by a conjunction to form a single sentence. No comma is needed when what follows the conjunction is not an independent clause:

A dentist and her assistant discussed tooth care with the students, and they used Mr. Gross Mouth to illustrate the points. (A comma is needed before the conjunction at the start of the second independent clause.)

A dentist and her assistant discussed tooth care with the students and used Mr. Gross Mouth to illustrate their points. (No comma is used before *and* here because *and used Mr. Gross Mouth to illustrate their points* could not stand alone as a complete sentence—it's the second half of the compound predicate discussed . . . *and used* . . . and is not a clause by itself.)

Note that imperative clauses (such as those often used in recipes) are independent, even though the subject is implied. When linked by a conjunction, they should be separated by a comma:

Braise the meat for 10 minutes, and then remove it from the pan.

6. Use commas around non-essential (non-restrictive) words, phrases or clauses. (See Chapter 5, page 65.)

7. Use a comma between coordinate adjectives (that is, if you can reverse the adjectives and put *and* between them):

The long, narrow passage was hard to navigate. (*Long* and *narrow* are coordinate adjectives in this sentence because you could write them as *narrow, long* and put *and* between them instead of the comma.) Adjectives referring to colors or ages are not considered coordinate with other adjectives and do not take commas:

The story of the old yellow dog is a sad one.

8. Use a comma before the adverbs *too, as well* or *also* at the end of a sentence:

Roberto Dumas came to the event, too.

9. Use commas to set off conjunctive adverbs (like *however, likewise, at the same time, therefore*) from the rest of the sentence (See Chapter 4, page 64):

Nitish, however, was early.

However, Nitish was early.

Nitish was early, however.

10. Use a comma to set off adverbial clauses beginning with *although, if, because* or *since* at the start of a sentence.

Although the police were criticized for the arrest, the chief defended it.

Because clouds covered the sky, it was difficult to see the comet last night.

11. Use a comma before *not* when showing contrast:

She said she thought independent voters preferred Stevens, not Malkowitz.

12. Use a comma to set off a noun of direct address:

John, could you come help me?

Never use a comma

In some instances, you should *never* use commas:

1. Never use a comma before a subordinate clause:

The game was called because it was raining. (*Because it was raining* starts with a subordinate conjunction and could not stand as a complete sentence, so there is no comma in front of it.)

2. Never use a comma between clauses that form part of a compound direct object.

Bridges said none of the workers required medical treatment and the leak did not pose a danger to public safety. (Think of it as: He said this and that. The clauses here are really part of a compound direct object. If we put a comma between them, the implication is that rather than Bridges saying the leak did not pose a danger, it is the reporter who is editorializing about the leak.)

My face is still slightly swollen, but my doctor says that is normal and I can get my hair done next week. (Again, the doctor is saying two things: *That is normal* and *I can get my hair done next week*. So, use no comma to separate the compound.)

The poll found that nine of 10 people believe smoking should be limited in public and eight of 10 believe employers should be allowed to limit smoking in workplaces. (No comma in this sentence because the poll found both things.)

3. Never use a comma before the conjunction at the end of a series unless it would be confusing without one. (See No. 3 in the list of instances in which commas are always used.)

4. Never use a comma between compound adjectives (that is, two words that team as one adjective, with one word describing the main adjective). Use a hyphen instead:

The sun beat brightly through a deep-blue sky the morning of the accident. (See the discussion of hyphens later in this chapter, page *91*.)

5. Never use a comma between adjectives when the second adjective is closely linked with the noun:

a new stone wall. (New and stone here are not coordinate adjectives—you cannot reverse them and put and between them. See No. 7 in the list of instances in which commas are always used.)

6. Never use a comma after a quotation mark. The comma, if needed, goes before the quotation mark:

"The beverage-container ordinance will probably be supported by the voters," MacDonald said.

7. Never use a comma after a period, exclamation point or question mark in a quotation when the sentence continues past it:

"Swim!" her father yelled.

8. Never use a comma before a partial or indirect quotation:

Feldman said "old-age blues" set in when he turned 30. (No comma after *said* because the quotation is not a complete sentence.)

9. Never use a comma around the abbreviations *Jr.* or *Sr.* after a name. (This is contrary to what you learned in English class, but it is the way journalists do it.)

10. Never use a comma before *Inc.* in a company name. (Another exception to your training in English classes.)

Possibly use a comma

Finally, here are two instances in which you *may* use a comma:

1. You may use a comma to separate a series of three or more short independent clauses:

"I came, I saw, I conquered."

2. You may use a comma to separate the same word used consecutively:

Whatever is, is.

SEMICOLONS

Semicolons aren't used much by journalists, but they do have some applications.

1. Use a semicolon between independent clauses when a conjunction is absent. (If there is a conjunction, use a comma instead of a semicolon. Don't put a semicolon in front of a conjunction.) Or you may make the two clauses separate sentences. What you should do depends on how closely related you think the clauses are and whether you think putting the clauses together would make the sentence too long:

The Padres are weak this year; they have the worst record in the league.

The Padres are weak this year. They have the worst record in the league.

Most journalists would prefer the period to the semicolon in that example, but if the two clauses contrasted with each other, many would probably use a semicolon:

Critics loved it; audiences stayed away in droves.

2. Use a semicolon before a conjunctive adverb connecting a sentence with two independent clauses (see Chapter 4, page *61*.):

Frome's lawyer contended he was mentally incompetent; however, the jury decided the evidence was not so clear.

Most journalists would rewrite this as two sentences:

Frome's lawyer contended he was mentally incompetent. The jury, however, decided the evidence was not so clear.

3. Use a semicolon between items in a series that has commas inside the items. Remember to put a semicolon here before the final conjunction.

The American flag is red, white and blue; the Canadian flag is red and white; and the West German flag is red, yellow and black.

Their diet consists of juice, toast and coffee for breakfast; fruit with yogurt, cottage cheese or tofu for lunch; and lean meat, vegetables and a starch for dinner.

COLONS

1. Use a colon to introduce a quotation of more than one sentence:

Baskins said: "As of now, there can't be a merger. We need more cooperation first between the city and county fire departments. We have to work together more."

2. Use a colon to introduce a list:

In other action, the commission:

—Approved Belle Kaufman's request that she be allowed to build a guest house in back of her home.

—Rejected the request by Ralph Hodges that a parcel of land he owns on Route YY be rezoned to allow him to build a dog-race track.

3. Use a colon to introduce a single-item summary or explanation with a dramatic pause:

He said you could summarize Jesus' message in three words: "Love thy neighbor."

If what follows the colon could stand alone as a complete sentence, as in that example, capitalize it; otherwise, do not.

4. Use a colon to take the place of *says* in a headline:

Jackson: "I want to be your president."

Some editors disapprove of this practice, but it's done in many newspapers.

5. Use a colon to introduce a subtitle:

Theodore Bernstein wrote "The Careful Writer: A Modern Guide to English Usage."

6. Use a colon to show time if it's not an even hour:

7:30 p.m.

7. Use a colon to separate chapter and verse in a citation of the Bible:

James 2:11

DASHES

1. Use dashes to set off a list or parenthetical material containing commas in the middle of a sentence:

The Jayhawks' defense—the linemen, the linebackers and the defensive backs—was exhausted after being pounded by the Sooner offense.

2. Use a dash for emphasis when a pause longer than a comma is needed:

He said he would do it—later. (Some editors say length of pause is not enough by itself—there also has to be a sharp turn of thought.)

3. Use a dash after a dateline or the wire-service credit in a newspaper story.

LONDON—

NEW YORK (UPI)—

NEW BLOOMFIELD, Mass. (AP)—

4. Use a dash in front of the attribution in a *blurb* or *pull-quote*.

"Let's face it, Hearst started the Spanish-American War."
—Mayor Jonathan Richardson

5. A dash is used in many newspapers as a bullet introducing items in a list:

In other business, the City Council:

—Approved a $525,000 contract with James Bros. Construction Co. to reroof city hall.

—Refused to rezone a half-acre tract at 202 Trenton Place for construction of a neighborhood market.

—Approved the rezoning of 10 acres at Hinton and Market streets from single-family residential use to multiple-family apartments.

PARENTHESES

Parentheses are used to set off asides, such as non-essential information or words inserted to clarify a quotation. If the aside contains at least one complete sentence, the period at the end is put inside the parentheses. If not, it goes outside:

He said his favorite movie was "La dolce vita" (The Good Life). (*The Good Life* is not a complete sentence, so the period comes after the parentheses. This aside, however, contains at least one complete sentence, so the period at the end of this sentence is inside the parentheses.)

Generally, though, journalists don't use parentheses but substitute commas instead. The idea is that it is best to avoid parentheses when possible because they can make writing look too complicated.

ELLIPSES

Ellipses (. . .) are used to indicate that something is not being quoted in its entirety, that something is missing. Most journalists seldom use ellipses, though, for fear they would make news stories look too much like a term paper. They *should* be used, however, when something is left out of the middle of a quoted sentence—otherwise you are rewriting quotations and misquoting people.

When whole sentences are left out of quotations, ellipses follow the space after the period of the previous sentence. An example:

"I've wanted to play pro basketball since I was a kid. . . . I always knew I'd make it."

Alternatives preferred by most journalists to get around ellipses are using *partial quotations* (quoting phrases rather than whole sentences) or putting transitions or attribution between the parts of the quotation.

QUOTATION MARKS

1. Quote only the exact words a speaker or text uses—not paraphrases. The word *said* does not necessarily indicate that the words listed are quoted—they may be paraphrased:

The president said the new bomber would be built next year. (Do not insert quotation marks.)

2. Don't misplace quotation marks in relation to other punctuation at the end of quotes:

• Periods and commas always go *inside* the quotation marks.

"Prohibitions against doctors' advertising is unfortunate," Rhysburg said, "because we end up with uneducated patients."

• Semicolons and colons always go *outside* the quotation marks. (AP makes an exception if they are part of the quoted material, but in practice this exception never seems to be observed—probably because it would look so odd to put a semicolon or colon inside the quotation marks at the end of a quote.) Example:

Nixon said, "I am not a crook"; others weren't so sure.

Fredericks spoke with pride of his "future farmers": his sons, Chris and Sam, and his daughter, Jane.

• Question marks and exclamation points go inside the quotation marks if they are part of the quotation, outside if they are not:

Have you read Ezra Pound's "Cantos"? (The question mark is outside the quotation mark because it is not part of the title.)

"Darn it!" she yelled. (The exclamation mark is inside the quotes because it is part of the quotation; the person said the statement with strong emotion.)

3. Don't use a quotation mark at the end of a *full-sentence quote* if the quotation is continued at the start of the next paragraph:

Peters said: "I'm upset by the whole situation.

"I didn't know what I was getting into, when I came here."

4. Do put a quotation mark at the end of a *partial quote* if it's continued at the start of the next paragraph:

Peters said he was "upset by the whole situation."

"I didn't know what I was getting into," he said.

5. Don't follow the rules for titles that you learned in English class when writing for a newspaper. Many newspapers use quotation marks around all titles except for those of magazines, newspapers, the Bible and other sacred books, reference books and musical pieces with names such as Symphony No. 1 or Opus 23 rather than ones like "Symphonie Fantastique" or "Visage."

6. Don't draw attention to clichés by putting quotation marks around them.

7. Don't put quotations around the names of musical groups, dance companies or theater troupes:

The Beatles (not "The Beatles")

8. Single-word quotations generally don't need quotations—at that point, aren't you really paraphrasing? Sometimes, however, a single word may be so colored that it's worth quoting by itself.

He said he felt fine. (No quotation marks needed around *fine*.)

He said he felt "wondrous." (The word is unusual enough it could be quoted.)

9. Don't use a quotation mark in place of the words *inches* or *minutes.*

nine inches or nine minutes, not 9''

HYPHENS

1. Use a hyphen between compound adjectives that precede the word they modify:

Price is an out-of-state athlete.

But do not use a hyphen after *very* or an adverb ending in -*ly*:

This is an easily remembered rule. (Easily is an -ly adverb, so there is no hyphen.)

You would use a hyphen, however, in a compound modifier after any word ending in -*ly* other than an adverb, such as the adjectives *friendly, manly* or *timely*, or the noun *family*:

He described it as a *friendly-service company*.

Doctorian's is a *family-owned business*.

Also, remember that this rule applies only to modifiers that precede the word modified. Compare:

She was a *part-time* worker. (Part-time precedes the word it modifies, the noun worker.)

She worked *part time*. (Part time follows the word it modifies, the verb *worked*.)

He is a *4-year-old* boy. (*Four-year-old* precedes the word it modifies, the noun *boy*.)

He is *4 years old*. (*Four years old* follows the word it modifies, the pronoun *he*.)

It should be noted, however, that compound adjectives beginning with *well* are hyphenated, according to AP, even as predicate adjectives:

The new boy in school was described by his former teacher as well-adjusted.

2. Use a hyphen after some prefixes, especially when without one a vowel would be doubled (see the list in Appendix A, pages 200–217):

Pre-empt, re-elect

3. Use hyphens in suspensive cases involving a modifier that applies to several words:

She most enjoyed the 3- and 4-year-old children.

4. Use hyphens in place of *to* in odds, ratios, scores and vote tabulations:

The odds were 3-2.

She led by a 2-1 ratio.

The Royals beat the Cardinals 11-2 in the exhibition game.

The Senate voted 48-2 in favor of the amendment.

5. Use hyphens when fractions or numbers from 21 to 99 are written out:

eighty-seven, two-thirds.

APOSTROPHES

Remember, the bottom of the apostrophe always points to the left. If it points to the right, it's not an apostrophe but a single open quotation mark.

1. Use an apostrophe to show possession with nouns. (See the rules in Chapter 1, pages **14–15**.)

2. Use an apostrophe to show something has been left out in contractions.

don't, I'll, decade of the '80s, rock 'n' roll

3. Use an apostrophe to make the plural of a single letter or numeral.

A's, 1's

4. Use an apostrophe with a pronoun to form a contraction.

it's (it is)

who's (who is)

5. Do not use an apostrophe to form the possessive form of any pronoun except *one*:

one's

6. Do not use an apostrophe in place of the word *feet*:

10 feet, not 10'

DIAGONALS

1. Use a diagonal to form a fraction or mixed number if your keyboard does not have a single key for the fraction:

1/10, 2 1/2.

2. Do not use diagonals with expressions such as *and/or, c/o, either/or* or *his/hers* except in quoted material. Instead, it is better to avoid *and/or* and *either/or* altogether and to write out *in care of* and *his or hers*.

Part Two

THE FUNDAMENTALS OF USAGE

Grammar provides a framework for good writing. Writing is effective only when communication takes place, and that occurs most efficiently when the writer, the editor and the reader understand the rules of grammar.

But good writing demands much more than good grammar. In "News Reporting and Writing," the Missouri Group lists six qualities of good writing:

1. It is precise.
2. It is clear.
3. It has a pace appropriate to the content.
4. It uses transitional devices that lead the reader from one thought to the next.
5. It appeals to the reader's senses.
6. It uses analogies.

The last four of those qualities relate to the way the writer weaves together information. Pacing is largely a matter of varying sentence lengths. Transitional devices lead the reader from one thought to the next. Appeals to the senses make the story come alive, and analogies provide a context for the reader to understand the material.

The first two—precision and clarity—relate directly to an understanding of grammar and its closely related cousin, usage.

Precision, in fact, is largely a matter of how well the writer uses words. A good writer will not use *less* when *fewer* is intended. Nor will that writer use *allude* when *refer* is intended.

Clarity, the Missouri Group writes, depends on three things:

1. Reliance on simple sentences.
2. Use of correct grammar and punctuation.
3. Thinking clearly.

In this section, we look at usage not as a grammatical problem but as a way of choosing words for precision and clarity.

First, we look at tightening—how to get your meaning across in fewer and shorter words, saving you space and the reader time, while making your expression more effective.

Then, we discuss choosing words that accurately express your meaning: getting idioms right and picking the right choice from among words that look alike, sound alike or have closely related shades of meaning.

Finally, we look at a contemporary problem of usage—avoiding unintended sexism, racism and similar forms of insensitivity.

CHAPTER 7

Tightening:
The Key
To Good Writing

The single most agreed-upon rule of good writing is that it should be concise. In "The Elements of Style," William Strunk and E.B. White write, "A sentence should contain no unnecessary words, a paragraph no unnecessary sentences, for the same reason that a drawing should have no unnecessary lines and a machine no unnecessary parts."

Saving words makes writing clearer and more effective, saves space and saves the reader's time. In "On Writing Well," William Zinsser says, "Writing improves in direct ratio to the number of things we can keep out of it that shouldn't be there."

It's the mark of the inexperienced writer to hold every word sacred, as jealously guarded against red-penciling as a drop of holy water against spilling. But Robert Louis Stevenson knew that conciseness is one of the differences between mere scribbling and art. "There is but one art," he wrote: "to omit." He added, "A man who knew how to omit would make an Iliad of a daily paper."

Studies show that typical business reports, letters and instructions can be made clearer and more effective by shortening them 20 to 30 percent. As Edwin Newman notes in his book "Strictly Speaking," "Business puts enormous pressure on the language. . . . Triple and quadruple phrases come into being—high retention characteristics, process knowledge rate development, anti-dilutive common stock equivalents. Under this pressure . . . adjectives become adverbs; nouns become adjectives; prepositions disappear; compounds abound."

Not only business is to blame; the problems can be found in all types of writing. Zinsser warns us to avoid what he calls "creeping nounism," which he defines as "a new disease that strings two or three nouns together when one will do." An example: "It no longer rains; we have precipitation activity." You also may recall a television ad for Bufferin that boasts of "protection ingredients." Most bureaucratic and technical jargon fits this pattern of two or more nouns in a row. It's better writing to find a shorter, everyday word that says the same thing more straightforwardly.

Of course, anyone can discard words, especially in someone else's writing. What's harder is knowing which words are the dead limbs, the pruning of which will help the tree grow stronger. And there's the clue. Brevity in itself may or may not be a virtue, just as pruning may improve a plant or kill it, depending on the skill of the gardener.

So let's be more precise than saying brevity is a worthy end in itself. The real virtue is not brevity but *conciseness*, which is brevity *and* completeness.

Calvin Coolidge's wife learned that when she asked him what the preacher had spoken about at church. "Silent Cal" replied, "Sin." When his wife then asked, "Well, what about it?" he answered, "He was against it." That's brevity but not conciseness; Coolidge's report is frustratingly incomplete.

The point is this: Don't just be brief; be complete—as briefly as possible.

HOW TO SAVE WORDS

Cut redundant or irrelevant words, phrases, clauses, sentences, paragraphs, sections or chapters. Get rid of details, examples, quotations, facts or ideas that don't add anything.

If there is a way to say something just as clearly in fewer words, choose the shorter way. If the number of words would stay the same but you could say it in shorter words, choose the shorter way. See the lists of windy phrases and pompous words at the end of this chapter for examples.

Here are some specific suggestions:

1. **Use exact parts of speech**:

   - Use a specific noun or verb without a modifier rather than a general noun or verb with a modifier. Don't write *a small city in Utah* when you could write *Cedar City, Utah*.

   - Use specific verbs rather than vague ones. For example, change *go* or *move* to *walk, run, jump, skip, hop* or *gallop*. Change *get* to *obtain, procure, attain* or *achieve*. But do so only when the meaning is enhanced by the more specific word; used appropriately, *go* and *get* are excellent words.

- Use shorter words when that makes sense, and use Anglo-Saxon verbs rather than Latinate ones. So, *say*, don't *state*; *drink*, don't *imbibe*; *use*, don't *utilize*.

Shorter English words often are derived from the Anglo-Saxon, the longer ones from Latin. Shorter words are more effective not only because less is more in art but also because they tap the primitive roots of the English language rather than the more abstract influence of Latin with its associations of scientific terminology. Because Anglo-Saxon words are more powerful, they often are used as off-color or swear words, while Latin words are acceptable. *Fart*, for example, would be considered crude, while the Latin *flatus* is socially acceptable, although somewhat obscure.

Notice that jargon phrases lean heavily on Latin, street language on Anglo-Saxon. But that doesn't mean short words aren't apt for grand statements. In Lincoln's 701-word second inaugural address, 505 of the words are one-syllable and 122 two-syllable. Similarly, short passages don't necessarily pack less wallop. According to The New York Times, the Lord's Prayer contains 56 words, the 23rd Psalm 118 words, the Gettysburg Address 226 words and the Ten Commandments 297 words. In contrast, the U.S. Department of Agriculture's directive on pricing cabbage contains 15,629 words.

- Avoid nouns that are so vague they say next to nothing. These words should be avoided when possible; look for something more specific: *area, aspect, concept, condition, consideration, factor, indication, infrastructure, parameter, phase* and *situation*.

- Use single verbs rather than verb phrases when possible. Generally, a verb phrase is wordier and less succinct than a single strong verb. Look for ways to emphasize the verb, particularly with *give, make* and *have*. Some examples:

    give consideration to: consider
    give encouragement to: encourage
    give instruction to: instruct
    have got: have
    have need for: need
    have the belief that: believe
    is reflective of: reflects
    is representative of: represents
    make adjustments: adjust

make an approximation: approximate
make mention of: mention
make out a list of: list
make the acquaintance of: meet
put emphasis on: emphasize

- Similarly, use simple, single adjectives, adverbs and prepositions and eliminate wordy phrases that mean the same thing:

a great deal of: many
all of a sudden: suddenly
as a consequence of: because
at an earlier date: previously
at the conclusion of: after
at the time when: when
despite the fact that: though
have a need (preference) for: need (prefer)
in large measure: mainly
in the not-too-distant future: soon
on a few occasions: occasionally
over a period of years: for years
while at the same time: while

- Avoid wordy euphemisms:

half a hundred: 50
maintenance engineer: janitor, custodian
reading material: books, pamphlets, etc.
resource center: library
waste-disposal personnel: sanitation workers

- Use verbs rather than noun phrases. Instead of writing *Prior to the Kissinger Committee investigation . . .* , write *Before the Kissinger Committee investigated . . ."*

- Avoid *-ize* verbs. They're often no more than pretentious jargon. For example, change *finalize* to *end* or *complete, institutionalize* to *put in an institution* or *make part of the institution, personalize* to *make more personal, prioritize* to *rank* and *utilize* to *use.*

  Don Ranly, a language expert and journalism professor at the University of Missouri, says, "If we don't quit utilizing the English language, we're going to finalize it."

- Avoid verbs that people try to turn into nouns: *activation, fabrication, maximization, optimization, rationalization* and *utilization.*

- Look out for verbs beginning with *re-*. Something is not *reaffirmed, redoubled* or *reshuffled* unless it already has been *affirmed, doubled* or *shuffled.*

- Get rid of *to be* verbs when possible. Frequently, they just detract from a more active verb. For example, change *he is hopeful that . . .* to *he hopes*; change *will be a participant in* to *will participate in*; change *it is my intention* to *I intend*; change *is productive* to *produces.* Forms of the verb *to be* occur frequently in sentences beginning with *there, here* or *it.* Instead of *It was Thoreau who said . . .* write *Thoreau said . . .*

- Use active voice instead of passive. Passive voice is wordier and less direct, and therefore less forceful. Write *Police shot a 13-year-old boy* not *A 13-year-old boy was shot by police.* An exception is when the person being acted upon is more important than the person doing the acting: *President Kennedy was shot today by an unknown gunman.*

2. Avoid *pleonasms*—words so lacking in specific meaning that they can be eliminated without changing what a sentence says—and other unnecessary words:

- Frequently, such words are vague modifiers like *a lot, kind of, perhaps, quite, really, somewhat, sort of* and *very.*

  These words are sometimes called "weasel words" because they are favorites of people trying to weasel their way out of taking a clear stand. Accepting evasiveness, like accepting pretentiousness or sentimentality, pollutes your writing.

  Even if you are trying to be honest, the use of such words *appears* at worst deceitful, at best wishy-washy. Look at this statement by Herbert G. Klein, President Nixon's director of communications: "There has been this feeling that perhaps the government's lying."

  As William Zinsser says: "Every little qualifier whittles away some fraction of trust on the part of the reader." Zinsser wants "writers who believe in themselves and what they are saying. Don't diminish this belief. Don't be *kind of* bold. Be bold."

- Pleonasms sometimes are doubled prepositions (*off of* for *off*) or prepositions that aren't needed at all (the *up* in *heading up*). In the sentence *She headed up the largest company in town* the *up* isn't necessary. (In this sentence, however, it is: *They headed up the mountain trail.*) Other examples of verbs that don't need *up*: *count, divide, drink, eat, fold, free, gather, heat, hoist, hurry, polish, rest, rise, settle.*

- Technical, business and academic writing is full of unnecessary phrases beginning with *in* or *the* and ending with *of* that can be cut: *(in) the amount of, (in) the area of, (in) the case of, the concept of, the factor of, (in) the field of, the idea of, (in) the process of, in terms of.*

- *The conjunction that* is frequently unnecessary: He said *that* he would. A general rule: If getting rid of *that* wouldn't change the meaning, get rid of it. Thus: *He said he would.* But *that* is necessary when:

   a. A time element, such as a day, comes between the verb and the dependent clause: *He said Tuesday* **that** . . .

   b. It follows one of these verbs: *advocate, assert, contend, declare, estimate, make clear, point out, propose* or *state.*

   c. It comes before a dependent clause beginning with one of the following conjunctions: *after, although, because, before, in addition to, until* or *while.*

- Avoid these windy substitutes for simpler conjunctions:

   as a consequence of: because
   as a result of: because
   assuming that: if
   at the time when: when
   at which time: when
   despite the fact that: though
   due to the fact that: since, because
   during the time that: while
   for the reason that: since, because
   in view of the fact that: since, because
   on the grounds that: since, because, as
   on the occasion of: when

- *Which is, who are* and *who is* can often be cut. Rewrite *The movie, which is a comedy . . .* as *The movie, a comedy . . .* Rewrite *The students who are attending . . .* as *The students attending . . .*

3. Avoid *redundancies* (needless repetition) whether in the same or different words.

- *Tautologies*—phrases that tell us something is what we already know it to be—are frequent examples. In phrases like *12 noon, personal friend, sad mourners, blue in color, true fact, armed gunman* and *completely destroyed,* one word implies the other, which is therefore unnecessary. Words like *famed, famous, renowned* and *well-known* likewise are unnecessary if the person or thing described is indeed famed, famous, renowned or well-known.

- The adjectives *both* and *different* often add nothing. What's the difference between *both John and Bill* and *John and Bill?* Between *three different views* and *three views?*

- The conjunction *whether* doesn't need to be followed by *or not* since it includes both possibilities.

4. In news stories, avoid modifiers that could suggest bias. For example, to say something "costs *only* $10" is to make a value judgment. To say "a bill *still* hasn't passed" proclaims you think it has taken too long. To say a candidate "*effectively* answered her opponent's charges" is to take sides. To say "*the fact that* he never had a chance" is to assert as a fact something that isn't necessarily so. Such words are judgmental; they also are space-wasters.

5. Avoid *clichés*. Although they are often succinct—that's why they caught on—clichés are wasted words because they are stale expressions rather than fresh ones: *quick as a cat*, *green as grass*. See the list of clichés at the end of this chapter, and learn to recognize them.

6. Avoid *prolixity*—giving more details than necessary. This sentence, for example, probably tells the reader more than he or she wants to know: *Sandy Hook is a tiny community of about 30 people, give or take five or six, and probably a classic example of a town with the welcome sign on one side of the post and the goodbye sign on the other*. But learn the difference between prolixity and color. The passage above may be inappropriate in a breaking news story but appropriate if the writer is setting a scene in a feature story.

7. Know your audience. You may be able to write or edit one way for a highbrow publication like The Chronicle of Higher Education, but an entirely different style and vocabulary would be necessary for readers of the New York Daily News.

8. Know when to be informal and when to be formal. Even in the same newspaper or magazine, different writing styles are permissible. A feature story may make liberal use of contractions, but a more formal news story may not be a good place to use them. Similarly, a liberal sprinkling of quotations may be desirable in a personality profile but less desirable in an editorial.

AVOIDING POMPOUS WORDS

Never use a big word when a smaller one will do. This list is a compilation of frequently used pompous words, including some that can be deleted and others that should yield to more appropriate or simpler substitutes. Remember, though, that on some occasions a word that often is used pompously may be appropriate and more precise.

Pompous words to eliminate or avoid

activity
area of
aspect
basis
case
character
essentially
ever (after *seldom* and *rarely*)
experience (v.) (Instead of "Are you experiencing pain?" try "Does it hurt?")
fairly
forthwith
greatly
hereby, herein, hereto, herewith
issue

level (Instead of "She teaches on the college level," try "She teaches college.")
nature
ongoing
operations
problem
process
proposition
question
situated (in)
situation (as in *classroom situation*, *crisis situation*)
therein, thereof, thereon
throughput
watershed

Pompous words to replace

accelerate: speed
accomplish: do
accord: grant
achieve: do
acquire: get
advent: arrival
affirmative: yes
aforementioned: this, that, these, those
albeit: but
amidst: amid
appears: seems
arise: get up
ascertain: find out
assist: help, aid
attempt: try
coequal: equal
cognizant: aware
commence: begin, start
communication: letter, memo

competency: competence
complete: fill out, finish
consult: ask
consummate: finish
contribute: give
contusion: bruise
currently: now
deceased: dead
deem: think, believe, judge
dentifrice: toothpaste
depart: leave
desire: wish, want
determine: find out
disclose: show
donate: give
dwell: live
edifice: building
educationist, educator: teacher
effectuate: cause

elect: choose, pick
employment: job
encounter: meet
endeavor: try
enhance: add to, improve
ensuing: following
execute: sign
exhibit: show
expedite: speed
eyesight: sight
facilitate: ease
facilities: buildings, space
failed to: did not
feasible: possible
finalize: finish, complete, end
firstly: first
forward: send
furnish: send
imbibe: drink
implement: do
in lieu of: instead of
inaugurate: begin, start
inconvenience: trouble
incursion: invasion
indicate: show
indignant: upset
individual: person, man or woman
inevitable: sure
inform: tell
initial: first
initiate: begin, start
input: opinion, suggestion
inquire: ask
insufficient: not enough
interface: connect
interrogate: question
inundate: flood
irregardless: regardless
laceration: cut, gash
language (v.): talk, speak, write
locate: find
massive: big, large
materially: much
maximize: increase
meaningful: big, important
minimize: lessen
modicum: some
necessitates: calls for
negative: no

numerous: many
obtain: get
oftentimes: often
optimistic: hopeful
orient: adjust
orientate: orient, or better still, adjust
output: production
overview: review, survey
party: person
per: a
peruse: read, examine
physician: doctor
place: put
pocketbook: purse
ponder: consider
populace: people, population
position: job
possess: own
presently: soon
primary: first, main
prohibit: forbid
provide: give
purchase: buy
purloin: steal
pursuant to: about
receive: get
regret: are sorry
remainder: rest
remark: say
remunerate: pay
requires: asks for, calls for, needs
reside: live
residence: house, home
respond: answer
retain: keep
reveal: show
rise: get up
secondly: second
self-confessed: confessed
spouse: husband, wife
states: says
submit: send, give
subsequent: later
substantial: big, great, large
substantially: largely
sufficient: enough
supply: send
sustain: suffer
terminate: stop, end

thirdly: third
thrust: main idea
ultimate: final, last

updated: current
utilize: use
vehicle: car, truck

AVOIDING WINDY PHRASES

Words can be pompous, and so can phrases. Even when phrases aren't pompous, they may not be the most economical and efficient way of conveying a thought. Never use more words than are necessary. Some examples:

Windy phrases to eliminate

a distance of
a period of
and/or
as a matter of fact
as already stated
as of this date
as per
as you are aware
at present, at the present time
at this point in time
contingent upon
frame of reference
fullest possible extent
goes without saying
in a very real sense
in fact
in my opinion
in question
in terms of
in the final (last) analysis
in the shape of

indeed
it appears (seems) that
it goes without saying
it is interesting to note that
it should be noted that
it stands to reason
it would appear that
needless to say
of course
the area of
the fact is
the fact that
the field of
the month of
the truth is
to be sure
to summarize the above
which is
who are
who is
you know

Windy phrases to replace

REDUNDANCIES

absolute guarantee (or perfection)
absolutely complete (or essential)
accidentally stumbled
acres *of land*

actual experience (or facts)
acute crisis
adequate enough
advance planning or reservations
adverse weather *conditions* (bad weather)
all *of*
all throughout
all-time record
another *additional*
appreciate (or depreciate) *in value*
attach (collaborate, collect, combine, gather) *together*
autopsy *to determine the cause of death*
awkward predicament
badly decomposed body (if long dead)
bare or *basic* essentials
basic fundamentals
big *in size*
blame *it on*
blazing inferno
both alike
brief *in duration*
brutal slaying (beating, murder, rape)
chief protagonist
circle (or skirt) *around*
coming future
common accord
commute *back and forth*
complete chaos (monopoly, overhaul)
completely demolished (destroyed, done, eliminated, empty, finished, full, surrounded, true, untrue)
concrete proposals
consensus *of opinion*
consequent result
dead body
deadly poison
definite decision
descend *down*
desirable benefits
died *suddenly*
downright lie
duly noted
early beginnings
early *hours*
Easter *Sunday*
eliminate *altogether*
enclosed *within*
end product (or result)
entirely complete (new, original, spontaneous)
exact counterpart (duplicate, facsimile, replica)

exactly identical
ever *before*
ever since
fatal killing
few *in number*
filled *to capacity*
final completion (conclusion, ending, outcome, result)
first annual (or ever)
first began (commenced, initiated, started)
first priority
flatly rejected
follow *after*
foreseeable future
free *and open to the public*
free gift (or pass)
free *of charge*
freewill offering
fresh beginning or start
frown (or smile) *on his (or her) face*
fully clothed
funeral *services*
future plans (or prospect)
gainfully employed
general public
general rule
generally agreed
gradually weaning
grand total
grateful thanks
great majority
ground rules
high noon
high technology
hot-water heater
hour of noon
important essentials
incumbent president (or governor, etc.)
interim *period between*
invited guest
Jewish rabbi
joint cooperation (or partnership)
learning experience
lonely isolation (or solitude)
low ebb
loyal Democrat (Republican, supporter)
main essentials
major breakthrough
many in number

married *her husband* (or *his wife*)
matinee *performance*
maximum *possible*
midway between
more preferable
most *all*
most unique
mutual cooperation
necessary *requisite*
new addition (beginning, bride, construction, creation, initiative, innovation, record, recruits)
newly created
noon luncheon
old adage (cliche, legend, maxim, proverb, veteran)
one of the last *remaining*
original source
own home
pair of (or *two*) twins
passing phase
past history
penetrate *into*
personal experience (or friend)
personally involved (or reviewed)
physical size
plan *ahead* (*for the future, in advance*)
postpone *until later*
qualified expert
radical transformation
raze *to the ground*
really unique
reason is because
recall (recede, refer, remand, retreat, revert) *back*
recur (repeat, resume, restate) *again*
reduce *down*
regular monthly meeting
resultant effect
results achieved
root cause
seldom *ever*
self-confessed
serious crisis (or danger)
short minutes
single unit
sink *down*
small *in size*
staunch supporter
still continues (persists, remains)
strangled *to death*

summer *months* (or *season*)
summoned *to the scene*
surrounding circumstances
sworn affidavits
temporary reprieve
total extinction or operating costs
totally demolished or destroyed
true fact
12 midnight or noon
ultimate conclusion (or end)
underground subway
underlying purpose
uniformly consistent
universal panacea
usual custom
utterly indestructible
viable alternative (option or solution); (Edwin Newman: ''If a solution isn't viable it's
    not a solution.'')
violent assault (or attack)
vitally necessary
watchful eye
worst *ever*
young juvenile

SPACE-WASTING VERB PHRASES

acted as chairman (chairwoman): presided
announce the names of: announce, identify
appeared on the scene: appeared
appoint to the post of: appoint
arrive at a decision: decide
assess a fine: fine
be acquainted with: know
be associated with: work with
be aware of: know
be cognizant of: know, notice
bring to a conclusion: conclude, end, finish
calm down: calm
came to a stop: stopped
check into (on, up on): check
close down: close
come to an end: end
commented to the effect that: commented that, said
comply with: follow, obey
conduct a poll: poll
continue on: continue
continue to remain: remain
costs the sum of: costs
debate about: debate

decide about (or on): decide, select
devoured by flames: burned
draws to a close: ends
drink down (or up): drink
empty out: empty
enclosed herein (or herewith): enclosed
enter a bid of: bid
enter in (or into): enter
exchanged wedding vows: married
face up to: face
favored to win: favored
file a lawsuit against: sue
give rise to: cause
give the nod: approve
had ought: ought
has got to: has to
has the ability (capability, talent) to: can
have an effect (impact) on: affect
have got to: must
include among them: include
infringe on (upon): infringe
is going to: will
know about: know
lose out: lose
made a speech (or statement): spoke
made an escape: escaped
made up (out) of: made of
makes one's home: lives
make contact with: meet, see
make inquiry regarding: ask about
make the acquaintance of: meet
participate in the decision-making process: have a say
passed away: died
pay off (or out): pay
perform a task: do
preceded in death: died earlier
present a report: report
promoted to the rank of: promoted to
protrude out: protrude
put into effect: start
raise motivation levels: encourage
referred to as: called
register approval: approve
register complaint (or objection): complain (or object)
register stamp of approval to: approve
resigned her position as: resigned as
revise downward: lower
rose to the cause (or defense) of: supported, defended

scored a gain: gained
seal off: seal
spell out: explain
sprung a surprise: surprised
started off with: started with
states the point that: states
stress the point that: stress that
succeed in doing: accomplish, do
take into consideration: consider
take place: happen
tendered her resignation: resigned
throw support behind: support
undertake a study: study
united in holy matrimony: married, wed
voiced objections: objected
was employed: worked
was in possession of: had
we wish to thank: we thank
went up in flames: burned
were scheduled to: would
win out: win

AVOIDING CLICHÉS

Like pompous words and windy phrases, clichés are an inefficient use of language—inefficient because they frequently can be
cut entirely or rewritten more economically. But even when they
seem the most concise way of expressing a thought, actually they
aren't. That's because clichés are phrases that have been used so
often they have lost their freshness and power. Using them dilutes
the originality of your work. When you feel tempted to use a cliché,
take the opportunity to invent a fresh phrase.

acid test
add insult to injury
after all is said and done
agree to disagree
all in a day's work
all things to all people
all too soon
all walks of life
almighty dollar
apple of one's eye
ardent admirers
armed to the teeth
as far as the eye could see

as luck would have it
at a loss for words
at a tender age
at long last
back in the saddle
beat a hasty retreat
beginning of the end
best left unsaid
better late than never
bewildering array
bitter end (or dispute)
blanket of snow
blazing inferno

blissfully ignorant
blood red
bloody riot
bolt from the blue
bombshell (announcement)
bonds of matrimony
bone of contention
breakneck speed
breathless anticipation
bring to a head
bring up to date
brute force
budding genius
burn the midnight oil
burning (desire, issue, question)
busy as a (beaver, bee)
But one thing is certain:
by hook or by crook
by leaps and bounds
calm before the storm
checkered (career, past)
cherished belief
Christmas come early for
cold as ice
colorful (display, scene)
concerted effort
conservative estimate
considered opinion
conspicuous by (his, her, its, their) absence
controversial (issue, person)
cool as a cucumber
coveted trophy
crack of dawn
cradled in luxury
crazy as a loon
crying (need, shame)
crystal clear
cutting edge
dashed the hopes
dastardly deed
dead as a doornail
deadly earnest
deciding factor
depths of despair
devouring flames
diamond in the rough
dig in their heels
do your own thing

dog tired
dotted the landscape
down to earth
drown your sorrows
easier said than done
eat, drink and be merry
eloquent silence
engage in conversation
every fiber of his being
eyeball to eyeball
facts and figures
faded dream
fall on deaf ears
far be it from me
far cry
fate worse than death
festive occasion
few and far between
fiery rebuttal
finger of destiny
finishing touch
fire swept through
flat as a board
fly in the ointment
follow in the footsteps of
food for thought
fools rush in
foot the bill
foregone conclusion
foul play
freak accident
frisky as a (kitten, pup)
from time immemorial
furrowed brow
gala (event, occasion)
game plan
generous to a fault
getting into full swing
given the green light
goes without saying
gory details
grave crisis
great lengths
great minds run in the same (channel, direction, gutter)
great open spaces
green light (as a verb)
hail of bullets
hale and hearty

hammer out
hand over fist
happy as a lark
hardy souls
hastily summoned
headache (when used to mean problem)
heap coals on the fire
heart of gold
heart of the matter
heartfelt thanks
heart's (content, desire)
hearty meal
heated argument
heave a sigh of relief
heavy as lead
Herculean efforts
hobbled by injury
hook, line and sinker
hot pursuit
hungry as a bear
immortal bard
in full swing
in high gear
in our midst
in the final analysis
in the nick of time
in the same boat
in this day and age
in this time frame
inextricably linked (or tied)
infinite capacity
iron out (difficulties, disagreements, troubles)
irons in the fire
it goes without saying
keeled over
labor of love
lashed out
last analysis
last but not least
last-ditch effort
leaps and bounds
leave no stone unturned
leaves much to be desired
left up in the air
legend in his (or her) own time
lend a helping hand

like a bolt from the blue
light as a feather
light of day
lion's share
lock, stock and barrel
long arm of the law
long years
lucky few
made a pretty picture
mantle of snow
many and various
marked contrast
marked improvement
matter of life and death
meaningful dialogue
meet head-on
meets the eye
method in his madness
miraculous escape
mixed blessing
momentous (decision, occasion)
monkey (on, off) (my, your, his, her, our, their) back(s)
motley crew
mourn the loss
mutually beneficial
name of the game
neat as a pin
need my space
needs no introduction
never a dull moment
nick of time
nipped in the bud
no easy answer
no place like home
no sooner said than done
none the worse (for wear, for the experience)
not to be outdone
official capacity
on a roll
no more than one occasion
one fell swoop
one of life's little ironies
only time will tell
open secret
opt for
order out of chaos

over and above
overwhelming (majority, odds)
own worst enemy
paid the penalty
painted a grim picture
pale as a ghost
paramount issue
permanent importance
part and parcel
patience of Job
paying the piper
picture of health
place in the sun
point with pride
powder keg (used as a metaphor)
pure as the driven snow
quiet as a mouse
rat race
red-letter day
reigns supreme
reins of government
reinvent the wheel
remains to be seen
remedy the situation
right stuff
ripe old age
road to recovery
rode roughshod over
rose to (new, the) heights
round of applause
rushed to the hospital
sadder but wiser
salt of the earth
sea of (upturned) faces
seamy side of life
seasoned observers (or reporters)
second to none
select few
selling like hot cakes
senseless murder
seriously inclined
shattering effect
shot in the arm
shrouded in mystery
sigh of relief
silhouetted against the sky
simple life
$64,000 question

slowly but surely
smart as a whip
smooth as silk
social amenities
something fishy
speak volumes
spearheading the campaign
spirited debate
spotlight the need
square peg in a round hole
staff of life
stern warning
stick to your guns
sticks out like a sore thumb
stinging rebuke
storms of protest
storm-tossed
straight-and-narrow path
stretches the truth
strong, silent type
stubborn as a mule
such is life
sunny South
superhuman effort
supreme sacrifice
sweat of his brow
sweeping changes
sweet 16
swing into high gear
take the bull by the horns
telling effect
there's the rub
this day and age
this (is, is not) a story about
thorough investigation
threw caution to the wind
through their paces
thunderous applause
time immemorial
time of one's life
tongue (firmly planted) in cheek
too numerous to mention
took to task
torrent of abuse
tower of strength
trapped like rats
trials and tribulations
true colors

turn thumbs down
uneasy (calm, truce)
unprecedented situation
untimely end
untiring efforts
up in arms
upset the apple cart
vanish into thin air
vast expanse
view with alarm
violence erupted
voiced approval
walk of life
warm as toast
watery grave

wealth of information
wear many hats
wee, small hours
weighty (matter, reason, tome)
whirlwind (courtship, romance, tour)
white as snow
widespread anxiety
winds of change
with bated breath
word to the wise
words fail to express
world-class
worse for wear
wrapped in mystery
writing on the wall

CHAPTER 8

Muddled Language

Idioms that are misunderstood and words that are confused or misused are common problems of the inexperienced writer. Both lead to a muddling of the language. Learning to avoid those problems is one of the keys to good communication.

Mistaken Idioms

Technically, an idiom is a common phrase that doesn't make sense when translated literally. More broadly, however, an idiom is any standard way in which words are joined in a language to express a thought.

So, idioms, like clichés, are common ways of saying things. Clichés are the words or phrases that editors tell you not to use; idioms are the ones you may use. But one person's idiom may be another person's cliché.

Nothing says you couldn't create your own expressions to take the place of idioms. But if you use idioms, make sure you write them correctly. Here are some that many people find confusing.

Wrong preposition

acquiesce to   *not* acquiesce with *or* in
as to   *not* as for
comply with   *not* comply to
contiguous to   *not* contiguous with
contrast to   *not* contrast with
convince of or that   *not* convince to
die of   *not* die with or die from
different from   *not* different than

dissent from   *not* dissent with
free from disease   *not* free of disease
identical with   *not* identical to
inculcate in or into   *not* inculcate with
independent of   *not* independent from
inflict on   *not* inflict with
instill into   *not* instill with
integrate with   *not* integrate into
investigation of   *not* investigation into
killed in (a wreck)   *not* killed after *or* killed following
persuade to   *not* persuade of *or* persuade that
plan to attend   *not* plan on attending
plead guilty of (a crime)   *not* plead guilty to
pleased (at, by) a gift   *not* pleased with a gift
put into words   *not* put in words
speak with   *not* speak to
talk with   *not* talk to

Other wrong words in a phrase

adopt a resolution   *not* pass
again and again   *not* over and over
any of the three   *not* either of the three
as good as   *not* equally good as
be sure to   *not* be sure and
compared with   *not* as compared with
decide whether   *not* decide if
doubt that   *not* doubt if
in halves or into halves   *not* in half
long illness   *not* extended illness
meeting took place   *not* meeting occurred (planned events take place; un-
   planned events occur)
on each side   *not* on either side
passed an ordinance   *not* adopted
range of actions   *not* range of action
red-haired person   *not* red-headed person (a person is red-haired; a bird
   may be red-headed)
safe-deposit box   *not* safety-deposit box
same thing   *not* same difference
short way   *not* short ways
suffer or sustain injuries   *not* receive injuries

Misunderstood meaning

Bobbsey twins: In Laura Lee Hope's novels, there were two sets of Bobbsey twins, each pair consisting of one boy and one girl; do not use to mean a pair of girls or a pair of boys.

chin up: means take heart; compare with *gin up*

desert island: not *deserted island*; *desert* as an adjective means barren and uninhabited

Hobson's choice: not a dilemma; means no choice at all

gin up: to get drunk; to enliven; compare with *chin up*

in behalf of: means in formal support of

inasmuch as: means in view of the fact that

insofar as: means to the degree that

like each other: use only if two are being compared

like one another: use only if more than two are being compared

lion's share: means all, not just most; in the Aesop fable, the lion got the whole thing, not just the majority

once removed: first cousins, once removed, are a generation apart; for example, your cousin's child is your first cousin, once removed; your cousin's child and your child are second cousins

pinch hitter: do not use except in baseball; not a mere substitute but someone put in to do a better job than the regular batter

raring to go: means eager, enthusiastic

strait is the gate: not *straight*; *strait* here means narrow

sustain a fatal injury: an injury is not sustained if it is fatal

there's no admission charge: better yet, just say it's free; avoid saying "there is no admission," which means nobody will be allowed to attend

to the manner born: not *manor:* "manner" is the spelling in Shakespeare's First Folio at the Folger Library

Errors with similar-sounding words

anchors aweigh   *not* anchors away

champing at the bit   *not* chomping

dog-eat-dog   *not* doggy dog

heart-rending   *not* heart-rendering

jerry-built   built poorly of cheap materials; *compare with* jury-rigged

jury-rigged   rigged for temporary use; *compare with jerry-built*

just deserts   *not* desserts

rapt in thought   *not* wrapt or wrapped in thought

razor strop   *not* strap

run a gantlet   *not* gauntlet
stamping grounds   *not* stomping
tinker's dam   *not* damn
toe the line   *not* tow
well-heeled   *not* healed
wet your whistle   *not* whet (means to moisten your mouth, not stimulate it)
whet your appetite   *not* wet (means to stimulate the appetite, not moisten it)
wrack and ruin   *not* wreak and ruin
wreak havoc   *not* wreck (considered by some a cliché anyway)

Grammatical errors

can only   *not* cannot help but
cannot help   *not* cannot help but
couldn't care less   *not* could care less
couldn't help   *not* couldn't help but
either . . . or   *not* either . . . nor
I hope   *not* I would hope
kind of movie   *not* kind of a movie
more important   *not* more importantly
neither is   *not* neither are
real good   grammatically, this idiom should be **really good;** *better still*, just
   say good
sort of book   *not* sort of a book
supposed to   *note* the d
used to   *note* the d

Confused Words

The English language is full of words that frequently are confused. Often, the confusion arises because the words sound alike;
sometimes it develops because of repeated misuse. Here is a list of
commonly confused words:

A

a while: Use when object of preposition: "It's been going on for quite *a
   while*." Also used in expressions like "a while ago" and "a while back."
awhile: the general adverb form: "It's been going on awhile."

abjure: to renounce
adjure: to entreat earnestly

abrogate: to annul
arrogate: to claim unduly

abstruse: hard to understand
obtuse: slow at understanding

abundant: plentiful
fulsome: excessive

accede: to agree reluctantly
exceed: to surpass

accelerate: to speed up
exhilarate: to stimulate

accept: to receive
except: but for

access: to enter
assess: to evaluate
excess: surplus

acetic: sour; acidic
aesthetic: artistic
ascetic: austere

act: a single thing that's done
action: something done that's made up of more than one act

ad: an advertisement
add: to derive a sum

adapt: to adjust
adopt, approve: to accept. You adopt or approve a resolution.
assume: You assume a role.
decide upon: You decide on a course.
pass: You pass a bill.

addition: something added on; the arithmetic process of making sums
edition: a version of a published work

adherence: support for
adherents: supporters

adventuresome: willing to take risks
adventurous: fond of adventure

adverse: unfavorable. Things are adverse.
averse: opposed. People are averse to things.

advice: noun
advise: verb

CONFUSED WORDS

affect: avoid as a noun, except in psychology to describe an emotion; as a verb means *to influence or produce a change in*

effect: as a noun means *result*; as a verb means *to cause or accomplish*

affluence: abundance
effluence: the process of flowing out
effluents: things that have flowed out, especially sewage

aggravate: to make worse. Only existing conditions are aggravated.
irritate: to make the skin itch
annoy: to bother

aid: help
aide: an assistant

ail: to be sick; to make sick
ale: a malt beverage

air: gas, atmosphere
e'er: ever (poetic)
ere: before (poetic)
err: to make a mistake
heir: an inheritor

aisle: a row
I'll: contraction for *I will*
isle: an island

alibi: a legal defense that one was somewhere else when a crime was committed
excuse: reason put forward to request forgiveness; except in a legal sense, this is generally the word you want

all ready: everyone prepared
already: by now

all together: everyone grouped
altogether: thoroughly

all ways: all methods
always: constantly

allowed: permitted
aloud: audibly

allude: not mention directly
elude: to evade
refer: mention directly

allusion: a casual mention
delusion: a mistaken belief, especially one caused by a mental disorder
elusion: an escape

illusion: an erroneous perception or belief
reference: a specific mention

almost: adv., nearly
most: adv., as in *most dangerous game*, or adj., as in *most people*

altar: sacred platform at the front of a church
alter: to change

alternate: the verb form; n., a proxy
alternative: n., a choice; adj., a substitute. Note that this is the only form to use as an adjective.

although: the preferred form at the start of a sentence
though: the only correct form at the end of a sentence

alumna: a woman who has attended a school (At some schools, graduation is implied.)
alumnae: women who have attended a school
alumni: men and women who have attended a school
alumnus: a man who has attended a school

amateur: non-professional
novice: a beginner

amend: to make a formal change
emend: to correct

amid: in the middle of something larger: "amid all that confusion"
among: surrounded by three or more separate things: "among the hungry of the world"
between: relationship involving only two or a number of things compared two at a time

amoral: outside of morality
immoral: in opposition to a moral code

amount: how much (weight or money)
number: how many (individual items)

ancestors, forebears: those from whom you are descended
descendants: those descended from you

anecdote: a short, amusing story
antidote: cure for a poison

ant: a kind of insect
aunt: sister of mother or father

anticipate: foresee with the possibility of forestalling
expect: foresee without necessarily being able to forestall

antiseptic: something that prevents bacteria from growing
disinfectant: something that destroys or neutralizes bacteria

CONFUSED WORDS

anxious: experiencing desire mixed with dread. One is anxious *about* or *for*.
eager: marked by enthusiasm and patience. One is eager *to*.

any: used with a choice among more than two
either: used with a choice between two

any more: something additional: "I don't have any more."
anymore: adverb

anyone: any person at all
any one: any single person or thing

anyway: in any event
any way: in any manner

apparent: connotes a doubt
evident: connotes existence of evidence

appose: to put side by side
oppose: to set against

appraise: to evaluate
apprise: to inform

apt: implies possibility
liable: implies an unpleasant probability
libel: written slander
likely: implies probability

arbitrate: to judge
mediate: to serve as a person who conciliates or reconciles

arc: a curve; something in that shape
ark: something offering protection

are: v., form of *to be*
hour: n., 60 minutes
our: pro., possessive form of *us*

area: amount of space
aria: operatic song for one singer

aroma: a pleasant smell
stench: a foul smell

arouse: to excite or stimulate
rouse: to stir or waken

arrant: downright
errant: straying

as: conj., introduces clauses
like: prep.; non-inclusive
such as: prep.; inclusive. "A book like this" means *not this one but another*;
   "a book such as this one" could mean *this one*.

as if: involves a condition
as though: involves a concession; often used mistakenly for "as if" when no concession is involved

ascent: climb
assent: agreement

assay: to test
essay: n., a short prose composition; v., to try

assert: to state as true
claim: a legal right; a justified demand

assignation: an appointment
assignment: an allotted task

assistance: help
assistants: helpers

assume: holding a hypothesis without proof
presume: believing without proof

assure: remove worry or uncertainty. People are *assured*.
ensure: to make an outcome inevitable. Events are *ensured*.
insure: to provide insurance. Objects or lives are *insured*.

astride: prep., with a leg on each side
bestride: v.; when you bestride a motorcycle, you are sitting astride it.

attendance: number attending; act of attending
attendants: people who attend

attorney: transacts business for you, legal or not; not a profession
lawyer: professional attorney in legal matters

auditions: are heard
trials or tryouts: are watched

auger: tool for boring
augur: to be an omen

aught: n., zero; adv., at all
ought: v., should

aural: pertains to the ear
oral: pertains to the mouth; spoken
verbal: pertains to language, spoken or written

autarchy: a totalitarian government
autarky: a policy of economic nationalism

avenge: v., to right a wrong
revenge: n., retaliation for satisfaction, not justice

average, mean: synonyms for the sum divided by the number of parts
median: the number with as many parts above as below

CONFUSED WORDS

range: the high minus the low

avocation: hobby
vocation: job, profession

avoid: to keep away from
avert: to turn away from
evade: to avoid by cleverness

B

bail: the money forfeited to a court if an accused person fails to appear at the trial
bale: a bundle, as of hay
bond: Bail is a form of bond, but to be specific, say someone ''posted bail'' or ''bail was set at'' instead of referring to bond.

baited: A hook or a witness or a bear is baited.
bated: Breath is bated, meaning abated.

balance: the credits minus the debits
remainder: a small part left over

ball: n., sphere
bawl: to cry

baloney: nonsense
bologna: a lunch meat

band: a combo; something that encircles and constricts
banned: barred

barbell: has adjustable weight
dumbbell: has fixed weight

baron: a nobleman
barren: infertile

base: n., foundation, a military headquarters, a bag in baseball; adj., lacking quality
bass: adj., low-voiced; n., a type of fish

bases: plural of base and basis
basis: main support

bazaar: marketplace
bizarre: odd

beach: n., sandy area; v., to run aground
beech: a kind of nut tree

beat: n., rhythm; v., to strike
beet: a kind of vegetable

because: preferred word for direct casual relationship

due to: Avoid using to mean *because*. If you do, the phrase should follow a form of *to be* and must modify a noun: instead of "He resigned due to ill health," write "His resignation was due to ill health."

since: a non-causal relationship

bellow: to shout

billow: to surge in waves

bemuse: as a verb means *confuse*; as an adjective means *engrossed in thought*; does not mean *amused* or *confused* as an adjective

confuse: to muddle or stupefy

berry: a small fruit

bury: to put under something

berth: a place of rest

birth: the emergence of something, especially living

beside: at the side of

besides: in addition to

best: for comparisons of three or more

better: for comparisons of two

bettor: one who gambles

bi: prefix normally meaning every two; biweekly means *every two weeks*.

semi: prefix meaning every half; semiweekly means *twice a week*.

biannual: twice a year

biennial: once in two years

bibulous: given to convivial drinking

bilious: ill-natured; suffering from liver problems

bight: inward curve in a coast; slack part of a rope loop

bite: v., action involving the teeth; n., a teeth wound, a mouthful

byte: computer term for one group of binary digits

blatant: conspicuous

flagrant: too obvious to ignore

blew: the past tense of blow

blue: the color

bloc: coalition with joint purpose or goal

block: cube; obstruction

blond: adjective for either sex; noun for male

blonde: noun for female

boar: a male hog

boor: an insensitive person

bore: n., someone who causes boredom; v., to drill

CONFUSED WORDS

board: v., to get on a ship; n., a plank
bored: v., made a hole in; adj., experiencing ennui

boarder: lodger who takes meals
border: boundary

boat: small, open vessel; exception: *U-boats*, which were submarines
ship: seagoing vessel larger than a boat

bold: fearless
bowled: past tense of to bowl

bolder: adj., more bold than
boulder: n., a big rock

bole: a tree's trunk
boll: a seed pod

born: to have been given birth
borne: to have given birth to; to have put up with; to have carried

borough: a walled town
borrow: to be lent something
burro: an ass
burrow: a hole in the ground; to dig

bough: n., a branch
bow: n., forward part of a boat, a loop, an archer's weapon; v., to bend in respect

bouillon: broth
bullion: gold or silver ingots

boy: a young male
buoy: n., a floating marker; v., to lift up

Brahman: the Hindu caste; the cattle breed
Brahmin: an aristocrat

brake: v., to stop
break: v., to shatter; n., an interval

bravery: what someone has within
courage: what someone shows when tested

breach: violation, opening or tear
breech: bottom, rear or back
broach: to make a hole; to start a discussion
brooch: an ornament

bread: n., the food
bred: v., raised

breadth: width
breath: n., air taken into the lungs

breathe: v., to take air into the lungs

briar: a pipe
brier: a thorned plant; a root used for making pipes

bridal: pertains to a bride or marriage ceremony
bridle: what you put on a horse's head to restrain it; rigging on a kite

bring: to carry toward
take: to carry away

Britain: the country
Briton: the inhabitant

brunet: adjective for male or female; noun for male
brunette: noun for female

bunch: a number of inanimate objects
crowd: a number of people

burger: a hamburger
burgher: person who lives in a town

burglary: involves entering a building with the intent of committing a crime
robbery: stealing involving violence or the threat of violence
theft: stealing without violence or threat of violence

bus: vehicle (present participial form: busing)
buss: kiss (present participial form: bussing)

C

calendar: records dates
calender: machine for pressing cloth or paper
colander: a strainer

calk: cleat
caulk: to make watertight

callous: hardened emotionally
callus: hardened skin

Calvary: where Jesus was crucified (near Jerusalem); frequently part of church names
cavalry: soldiers on horseback

can, could: is able; *could* is the past and conditional form of *can*
may, might: *might* is the past and conditional form of *may*; has permission; there is the possibility: "He may." Some say *may* implies that uncertainty still persists, while *might* refers to a possibility in the past; others say *might* is less definite than *may*

canapé: an appetizer
canopy: an awning

CONFUSED WORDS

129

CONFUSED WORDS

cannon: a gun
canon: church law

canvas: n., cloth used for tents
canvass: v., to visit to ask for something

capital: the city
Capitol: the building (note capital letter)

carat: a unit of weight; used with diamonds and other gems
caret: an editing mark inserting something
carrot: the vegetable
karat: a measure for the purity of gold (24 being pure)
karate: the martial art

careen: to sway (especially a boat or ship)
career: to move quickly, especially at full speed
carom: to rebound after striking

carousal: a drunken revel
carousel: a merry-go-round

cast: n., a group of actors, v., to throw
caste: a social class

caster: little wheel under furniture
castor: an ingredient in perfume; the name of the laxative oil: castor oil

casual: not formal
causal: pertaining to a cause

celebrant: participant or presiding official in a religious service
celebrator: participant in a non-religious celebration

celibate: unmarried; abstaining from sexual intercourse
chaste: morally pure; abstaining from sexual intercourse

cement: the powder in concrete
concrete: the rocklike substance of which roads, sidewalks and walls are
   made

censor: n., one who previews things to prevent others from seeing material
   deemed harmful; v., to censor
censer: an incense burner
censure: an official reprimand

centenarian: person older than 100
centurion: a Roman military commander

ceremonial: formal
ceremonious: overly concerned with formalities

cession: an act of granting, surrendering or transferring something
session: the term of a meeting

130

chaff: husks
chafe: to rub; to wear away by rubbing

Champagne: the province in France or the bubbly wine made there
champagne: the bubbly wine made in imitation of that made in Champagne
Champaign: the city in Illinois

chaperon: as a noun, a man or woman who accompanies as a guardian; the verb form
chaperone: only used to mean a woman and therefore should be excluded from modern usage

character: what a person is
reputation: what others think a person is

cheap: adj., inexpensive
cheep: v., to chirp

childish: immature; a perjorative term
childlike: maintaining the positive qualities of childhood

choose: present tense
chose: past participle

choral: adj., written for a choir or chorus
chorale: n., a choral composition
coral: n., substance built by sea creatures that forms a reef; adj., reddish pink
corral: n., a fenced-off area for horses

chord: harmonizing notes
cord: string or rope; unit of wood; part of the body: spinal cord

cite: to quote in support
sight: something seen; the sense
site: a place

citizen: one who shares in political rights of a nation. A person is a citizen only of a nation, not of a city, county, region or state.
resident: a person who lives in an area

civic: pertains to a city
civil: polite; society not military; laws not criminal; internal war

classic: n., something of the highest rank; adj., recognized for many years as a model
classical: adj., pertaining to a certain historical period, especially ancient Greece and Rome, or to serious music

clew: a ball of thread of yarn
clue: a piece of evidence; a hint

client: a person who uses the services of a professional
customer: a person who buys something

climactic: refers to a climax
climatic: refers to the weather

close: to shut, to end
clothes: garments
cloths: fabrics

coarse: rough, crude
course: class; series; division of a meal; field for a sport

collaborate: to work together
collude: to cooperate secretly to deceive
connive: to provide secret help or indulgence

collision: when two moving objects hit
crash: when a moving object hits something else, mobile or stationary

comic: n., a funny person
comical: adj., funny

commensurate: corresponding to
commiserate: to feel sympathy for
corroborate: to verify

common: shared; belonging to jointly
mutual: reciprocal; having the same relationship

compare to: to point out similarities
compare with: to point out similarities and differences
contrast: to point out differences and, perhaps, similarities, as well

complacent: satisfied
complaisant: obliging

complement: v., to complete by supplementing; n., that which supplements
    and completes
compliment: v., n., praise

complementary: supplying needs
complimentary: free; praise

compose: to create or put together. The whole is composed of the parts.
    Some editors insist that compose be used only in passive voice, but others
    permit it to be used actively to mean *constitute*.
comprise: to contain. The whole comprises the parts.
constitute: to form or make up. The parts constitute the whole.

comprehensible: understandable
comprehensive: complete

compulsive: obsessive
impulsive: spontaneous; based on whim rather than thought

concerned about: preoccupied
concerned with: engaged in

concert: requires two or more performers
recital: given by one performer

connotation: implied meaning or emotional flavor of a word or phrase
denotation: actual or literal meaning of a word or phrase

conscience: n., a moral sense
conscious: adj., awake
consciousness: n., awareness

consecutive: one after another without break
successive: one after another

consequent: following as a natural result; used when the events are related
subsequent: following; used when the events are not related

consul: diplomat
council: deliberative body; assembly of advisers
counsel: legal adviser; advice; to advise

contagious: transmitted by contact
infectious: transmitted by water, air, etc.

contemptible: deserving of scorn
contemptuous: showing or feeling scorn

continual: repeated
continuous: uninterrupted

convince: You convince *that* or *of*; some editors say you convince *yourself*; The Washington Post Deskbook says convince is "to win over by argument."
persuade: You persuade *to*; some editors say you persuade *others*; The Washington Post Deskbook says persuade is "to win over by appeal to reason or emotion."

core: center
corps: group of people
corpse: a dead body

co-respondent: a person in a divorce suit charged with commiting adultery with the person from whom the divorce is sought
corespondent: person accused with the defendant
correspondent: one who writes; that which matches with something else

council: see *consul*

councilor: member of a council
counselor: adviser; lawyer; aide at an embassy

country: the geographical territory
nation: the political entity

courage: see *bravery*

CONFUSED WORDS

courteous: kind beyond politeness
polite: having good manners

creak: v., to squeak
creek: n., a stream

credible: believable
creditable: worthy of approval, credit or praise
credulous: gullible

credulity, credulousness: synonyms

criteria: plural
criterion: singular

crochet: kind of knitting
crotchet: an odd fancy

croquet: lawn game
croquette: meat patty

cue: signal; billiard stick
quay: a wharf
queue: lineup

currant: n., kind of berry
current: n., flow; adj., present

customary: set by custom
habitual: set by habit
usual: ordinary

cymbal: percussive musical instrument
symbol: something that stands for something else

cypress: the tree
Cyprus: the country

D

damaged: means partial. Do not say "partially damaged" or "completely damaged."
destroyed: means complete. Do not say "partially destroyed" or "completely destroyed."
data: usually plural: "The data *have* been gathered" (many separate items); but occasionally singular: "The data *is* sound" (viewed as unit).
datum: singular

decease: die
disease: illness

defective: faulty
deficient: lacking

definite: certain, clear, fixed
definitive: thorough; a model

defuse: to stop
diffuse: to scatter

delude: to deceive
dilute: to water down

demur: v., to raise objections; n., an objection raised
demure: adj., quiet and serious

deny: to say something is false
dispute: v., to argue; n., an argument
rebuff: v., to snub; n., a snub
rebuke: v., to condemn for an offense; n., a reproof
rebut: to argue to the contrary
refute: to prove something is false

depositary: a person you entrust with keeping something safe
depository: a place where things are kept safe

depraved: corrupted
deprived: underprivileged

deprecate: to disapprove of
depreciate: to belittle or devalue

desert: n., barren region, also used in phrase "just deserts"; v., to abandon
dessert: n., sweet course in a meal

detract: to lessen; to take from
distract: to divert attention

device: noun
devise: verb

die: to lose life or to cut with a die; forms: *died, has died, is dying* (losing life), *is dieing* (cutting a die)
dye: to change color with a chemical; forms; *dyed, has dyed, is dyeing*

dinghy: boat
dingy: drab

disapprove: to express disfavor
disprove: to show something to be false

disassemble: to take part
dissemble: to conceal true feelings

disburse: to pay money
dispense: to deal out
disperse: to scatter or vanish

disc: phonograph record or compact disc; part of a plow

disk: any round, flat object; a computer disk; an anatomical structure

discover: to find something that was not seen before
invent: to create something

discredit: to destroy confidence in
disparage: to belittle

discreet: adj., prudent
discrete: adj., separate

disinterested: impartial (may be interested but neutral)
uninterested: indifferent (lacking interest)

distinct: unmistakable
distinctive: unique
distinguished: excellent

divers: adj., several; n., people who dive in the water
diverse: different

dock: a large excavated basin used for receiving ships between voyages
pier: platform extending from shore over water
wharf: platform parallel to a shore

don: to put on (a garment)
doff: to take off (a garment)

done: past participle of do
dun: v., to annoy, as for payment of a debt; adj., grayish brown

dose: an amount of medicine
doze: to nap

doubt that: used in negative statements and questions
doubt whether: used in positive statements indicating uncertainty as to options

dribble: v., to bounce a ball
drivel: nonsense

drier: adj., less moist
dryer: n., device for drying things

drunk: adj., used after verb *to be*
drunken: adj., used before nouns

dual: composed of two
duel: fight between two people

due to: see *because*

E

each other: involving two
one another: involving more than two

eclectic: drawing on a variety of sources
electric: operated by electricity
electrical: pertains to electricity
electronic: produced by a flow of electrons in vacuum tubes, transistors, microchips

ecology: the science of the relationship between organisms and environment
environment: surroundings

economic: pertains to finances
economical: thrifty

eek: an exclamation
eke: to get with difficulty

effective: having an effect
effectual: true to its purpose
efficacious: produces the desired effect
efficient: competent; productive

egoistic: self-centered
egotistic: boastful

elder, eldest: used with people
older, oldest: used with things or people

electric: see *eclectic*

elegy: a sad song or poem
eulogy: a funeral oration

elicit: to draw out
illicit: prohibited

eligible: open to be chosen
illegible: indecipherable

elongated: increased in space
extended: increased in range
prolonged: beyond normal limits
protracted: extended needlessly to the point of boredom

emanate: v., to emit
eminent: adj., prominent
immanent: inherent in; present throughout the universe
imminent: about to happen

emerge: to come into view
immerge: to plunge into
immerse: to put completely into liquid

emigrant: one who leaves a county
immigrant: one who enters a country

CONFUSED WORDS

emigrate: to leave a country
immigrate: to enter a country

endemic: native
epidemic: rapidly spread

engine: large vehicles (ships, airplanes, rockets) have one
motor: small vehicles, boats and appliances have one. A car may be said to have either an engine or a motor.

enormity: wickedness
enormousness: vastness

entitled: deserving (of); gave a title to (active voice)
titled: designated by a title (passive voice); gave a title to (active voice)

entomology: study of insects
etymology: study of word origins

envelop: v., to surround; to cover
envelope: n., container for a letter

envisage: to imagine; to visualize
envision: to foresee; to visualize

epigram: a concise, clever statement or poem
epithet: a term characterizing someone or something
epitaph: a statement or inscription in memory of someone dead

equable: uniform
equitable: fair

equivalent: of equal value
equivocation: use of ambiguous terms to hide the truth

erasable: capable of being erased
irascible: quick-tempered

errant: misbehaving; traveling to seek adventure (see *arrant*)
erring: sinning; making mistakes

error: an inaccuracy
mistake: an error; a misunderstanding

eruption: a sudden, violent outbreak
irruption: a forcible entry; a sudden increase in animal population

eschatology: branch of theology dealing with death and judgment
scatology: obsession with excrement

especially: particularly; notably
specially: for a special purpose or occasion

ever so often: frequently
every so often: occasionally

every day: adv. Example: "editing *every day*"
everyday: adj. Example: "*everyday* editing"

every one: each single one
everyone: everybody

evoke: to call up or inspire emotions, memories, response, etc.
invoke: to call for the help of, as in prayer

exalt: to raise in rank; to praise
exult: to rejoice

exceedingly: extremely
excessively: too much

exceptionable: objectionable
exceptional: unusual

excite: to arouse emotionally
incite: to stir to action

exercise: to work out physically
exorcise: to drive out (as in driving out demons)

exhume: to dig up a corpse
exude: to radiate

expatiate: to elaborate
expiate: to atone for

expatriate: someone who has left a country to live elsewhere
ex-patriot: a former patriot

extant: adj., still existing
extent: n., range

F

facetious: merely amusing
factious: creating dissent
factitious: not genuine
fictitious: imaginary

faint: adj., weak; v., to swoon
feign: to pretend
feint: a fake attack

fair: n., a periodical exhibition; adj., just
fare: v., to progress; n., price to travel, passenger, food provided

faker: someone who engages in fraud
fakir: a holy man, especially a Moslem or Hindu who performs magic feats

farther: used with literal distance
further: used for figurative distance

fatal: resulting in death
fateful: deciding the fate of

faze: to disturb
phase: a stage of development

feat: a deed
feet: appendages on which shoes are worn
fete: a lavish party

feel: should be reserved for physical or emotional sensations
think: the proper term to use for mental activity

ferment: to undergo chemical conversion after adding a yeast
foment: to cause trouble

fewer: smaller in number; used for plural items
less: smaller in amount; used for singular items
under: use for spatial comparisons only

figuratively: in a metaphorical sense
literally: actually; often confused with figuratively

figurine: a representation up to two feet tall of a person or animal
sculptor: an artist who creates three-dimensional art
sculpture: any three-dimensional work of art
statue: a big representation of a person or animal
statuette: a representation from one to two feet tall of a person or animal

filet: a net or lace with a pattern of squares; also the spelling in filet mignon
   (other boneless strips of meat may be spelled either way)
fillet: a narrow strip (as of ribbon)

find: to discover
fined: penalized

fine: a penalty of money
sentence: a penalty of time. A convict is sentenced to five years and fined
   $5,000, not sentenced to five years and a $5,000 fine.

fir: a kind of evergreen tree
for: prep.
fur: the hair of an animal; a garment made from the hair of an animal

fiscal: financial
physical: pertaining to the body

flack: press agent
flak: anti-aircraft shells

flagrant: glaringly evident
fragrant: having a pleasant smell

flair: a talent

flare: n., a light; v., to start suddenly

flammable: preferred over inflammable by The Washington Post. Many other editors consider this an illiteracy.

inflammable: Use this rather than flammable when speaking of temperaments.

inflammation: the medical term

inflammatory: arouses emotions

flaunt: to show off

flout: to defy; to disdain

flea: n., the pest

flee: v., to leave

flew: past participle of fly

flu: influenza

flue: smoke duct in a chimney

flier: airman; handbill

Flyer: used in proper name of some trains and buses

flotsam: wreckage of a ship or its cargo floating at sea

jetsam: things jettisoned from a ship to lighten the load

lagan (ligan): jetsam attached to a buoy to make recovery easier

flounder: to struggle helplessly; a fish

founder: to sink or become disabled. First you flounder, then you founder.

flour: ground grain

flower: an open blossom

flowed: past participle of to flow

flown: past participle of to fly; often mistakenly used for flowed

forbear: v., to cease or to refrain from

forebear: n., an ancestor or forefather

forbid: you forbid *to*

prohibit: you prohibit *from*

forbidding: adj., difficult

foreboding: n., a prediction or portent; adj., ominous

forced: compulsory; strained

forceful: effective; full of force

forcible: involves use of brute force

forego: to precede

forgo: to go without; to relinquish

foregoing: preceding

forgoing: giving up; abstaining from

foreword: an introduction

forward: onward

formally: in a formal manner
formerly: previously

fort: an enclosure for defense
forte: n., a strength; adj., loud (Italian)

forth: adv., onward
fourth: place after the third

forthcoming: about to take place; willing to give information
forthright: frank

fortuitous: accidental; by chance
fortunate: lucky

foul: rotten
fowl: pertaining to birds

freeze: to form ice
frieze: a decorative band

fulsome: disgusting; insincerely excessive
fullness: abundance

furl: to roll up
furrow: n. wrinkle, rut in the soil; v., to wrinkle

G

gaff: a hook
gaffe: a blunder

gait: a way of walking
gate: an entrance

gamble: to wager
gambol: to frolic

gantlet: a flogging, as in "running a gantlet"
gauntlet: a glove, as in "throwing down a gauntlet"

gender: grammatical term for whether a word is masculine, feminine or neuter
sex: describes whether a being is male or female

genteel: affectedly elegant
gentile: to Jews, anyone not Jewish; to Mormons, anyone not Mormon.
gentle: not rough

gibe: to taunt
jibe: to conform; to change course
jive: to kid; to talk lingo

gild: v., to cover with gold
guild: n., a union

glacier: ice field
glazier: person who puts glass in windows

glutinous: adj., like glue
gluttonous: adj., overeating

gorilla: the ape
guerrilla: the fighter

gothic: gloomy or fantastic, as in "gothic novel"
Gothic: all other uses

gourmand: a big eater
gourmet: a connoisseur of food

grate: a grill for holding wood in a fireplace
great: larger than normal

grill: n. metal bars for cooking meat or fish; v., to broil meat or fish, to question harshly
grille: a screen or grating, such as on the front of a car

grisly: gruesome
gristly: having gristles
grizzled: gray-streaked
grizzly: n., a gray bear; adj., gray

guarantee: n., a pledge to replace the product or refund the money if the product doesn't work; v., to make such a pledge
guaranty: n., a pledge to assume someone else's responsibility; a financial security
warranty: a pledge that something is true

H

hail: v., to greet, to acclaim after the fact; n., ice from the sky
hale: v., to take into court, to drag; adj., healthy

herald: to announce before the fact

hall: n., a large room
haul: v., to drag forcibly, to carry; n., booty, distance to be traveled

half brothers, half sisters: children with only one parent in common
stepbrothers, stepsisters: children related by the re-marriage of parents

half-mast: flags are lowered (not raised) to half-mast on ships and at naval stations only
half-staff: flags are lowered (not raised) to half-staff anywhere else

143

handmade: made by hand
self-made: made by itself. A millionaire may be self-made, but an antique is handmade.

hangar: aircraft shelter
hanger: as in "coat hanger" or "paper hanger"

hanged: executed
hung: put up

hapless: unfortunate
hopeless: lacking hope

hardy: bold, rugged. A plant that can survive under unfavorable conditions is hardy.
hearty: jovial; nourishing

heal: to recover from injury
heel: back of the foot; bottom of the shoe; crust of bread

healthful: conducive to health. Foods are healthful.
healthy: having health. Living things are healthy.

hear: to listen
here: at this place

heard: past participle of hear
herd: a group of animals

helix: a three-dimensional design
spiral: a two-dimensional design; exception: "spiral staircase"

heroin: the drug
heroine: a female hero

hew: v., to chop
hue: n., color

hippie: 1960s term for a "flower child"
hippy: having big hips

hire: to employ; to gain use of
lease: to grant or gain by contract, especially property
let: to grant by contract, especially property

historic: having importance in history
historical: concerned with history. A historic book made history, but a historical book is about it.

hoard: n., a storehouse; v., to store
horde: n., a swarm

holey: adj., full of holes
holly: n., a kind of plant popular at Christmas

holy: adj., sacred
wholly: adv., entirely

home: a home cannot be sold
house: a house can be sold

homicide: a slaying or killing
manslaughter: a homicide without premeditation or malice
murder: a malicious, premeditated homicide (or, in some states, one done while committing another felony). Do not call a killing a murder until someone has been convicted.

homogeneous: having the same structure
homogenous: having the same structure because of common descent

human: pertaining to people
humane: compassionate

hurdle: to jump
hurtle: to throw

hypercritical: too severe
hypocritical: pretending to be something you're not

I

ideal: a model; a goal
idle: not busy
idol: a worshipped image
idyll: a scene, poem or event of rural simplicity; a romantic interlude

if: introduces a conditional clause: "if a, then b"
whether: introduces a noun clause involving two choices (the "or not" is redundant). Although most authorities say *if* and *whether* may be used interchangeably, many editors still insist on the distinction.
weather: atmospheric conditions

imaginary: existing only in the imagination
imaginative: showing a high degree of imagination

immigrate: see *emigrate*

impassable: not capable of being passed
impassible: incapable of suffering or showing emotion

imperial: pertaining to an empire or emperor
imperious: domineering; proud

imply: to hint. Writers or speakers imply.
infer: to deduce. Readers or listeners infer.

imposter: one who levies a tax

impostor: one who pretends to be someone else

impracticable: said of a plan that's unworkable, an unmanageable person

impractical: said of an unwise plan, a person who can't handle practical matters

impugn: to challenge
impute: to attribute

impulsive: see *compulsive*

in behalf of: in informal support of
on behalf of: in formal representation of

in to: in and toward; preposition followed by an adverb
into: inside; preposition only

inapt: inappropriate
inept: incompetent

inasmuch as: in view of the fact that
insofar as: to the degree that

incidence: rate at which something occurs
incidents: the things that occur

incite: to arouse; see also *excite*
insight: a clear understanding

incredible: unbelievable
incredulous: skeptical

indeterminable: can't be determined
indeterminate: not fixed

indict: to charge with a crime
indite: to put into words

industrial: pertaining to industry
industrious: hardworking

inequity: unfairness
iniquity: wickedness

inert: lifeless; lacking motion
innate: inborn; inherent; natural

infectious: see *contagious*

inflammable: see *flammable*

ingenious: inventive
ingenuous: honest; forthright, perhaps to the point of naivete

insistent: demanding
persistent: continuing firmly

insoluble: can't be dissolved
insolvable: can't be solved
insolvent: can't pay debts

instinct: a non-thinking, automatic response of animals
intuition: knowledge gained without conscious reasoning

interment: burial
internment: a detention

interstate: between states
intestate: not having a will
intrastate: within a state

it's: contraction for "it is." (Some also permit it as a contraction for "it has.")
its: possessive form of "it"

J

jam: made from the whole fruit (usually not citrus fruit)
jamb: side of a doorway or window frame
marmalade: made from pulp and rinds of citrus fruit

judicial: pertaining to a judge or court
judicious: sound in judgment
juridical: pertaining to administration of justice

juggler: a person who juggles
jugular: a neck vein

K

knave: a rogue
nave: part of the interior of a church

knead: to mold
kneed: past participle of to knee
need: to require

knew: past participle of to know
new: recent

knight: a medieval soldier
night: part of the day after the sun has set

knit: to loop yarn to make a fabric
nit: a louse

know: v., to comprehend
no: adj., not any; adv., opposite of yes

CONFUSED WORDS

L

lam: an escape; as in "on the lam"
lamb: baby sheep

lama: a Tibetan monk
llama: the animal found in the Andes

languid: weak; sluggish
limpid: clear; calm

last: final (exceptions: last week, last month, last year)
latest: most recent, as in "latest letter" (not the final one)
past: most recent as in "past three years" (not the final ones)

laudable: praiseworthy
laudatory: expressing praise

lay: transitive v., to set down; principal parts: *lay, lay, have laid, is laying*
lie: intransitive v., to recline; principal parts: *lie, lay, have lain, is lying*
lye: n., a strong alkaline solution

leach: to separate a solid from its solution by percolation
leech: n., a bloodsucker; v., to suck blood

lead: n., metal; v., present tense of to lead
led: past tense of to lead

leak: v., to go through an opening; n., a hole
leek: n., a vegetable related to the onion

lean: v., to stand diagonally, as in resting against something
lien: the right to take or sell a debtor's property as security or payment on a loan

leased: past participle of to lease
least: smallest

leave alone: to depart from
let alone: to allow to be undisturbed

lectern: see *podium*

legislator: a lawmaker
legislature: a body of lawmakers

lend: the verb; past tense is "lent," not "loaned"
loan: the noun. Some authorities permit this to be used as the verb if what is lent is money, but you should avoid that usage to be on the safe side.

lone: adj., by oneself

less: see *fewer*

lessee: a tenant
lessor: landlord or one who grants a lease

148

lessen: v., to make less
lesson: n., an instruction

lesser: adj., smaller
lessor: n., a landlord

let's: contraction for let us
lets: allows

levee: a riverbank
levy· n., an imposed tax; v., to impose a tax

liable: legally responsible; should not be used to mean "likely" (see *apt*)
libel: v., defame; n., defamation
likely: probable

lichen: n., a fungus-like plant that grows on trees and roots
liken: v., to compare

lightening: making less heavy or dark
lightning: flash of light in the sky

like each other: two are alike
like one another: more than two are alike

linage: number of lines of printed material
lineage: descent from an ancestor

lineament: facial contour
liniment: a salve

liqueur: a sweet, flavored alcoholic drink
liquor: a distilled alcoholic drink

literal: actual
littoral: pertaining to a shore

literally: see *figuratively*

load: v., to pack; n., a pack
lode: a deposit of ore

loath: adj., reluctant; is followed by *to*
loathe: v., to dislike greatly

local: nearby
locale: site

located: set
situated: set on a significant site

loose: v., to unfasten; adj., not tight
lose: v., to fail to win; to fail to keep

luxuriant: abundant
luxurious: comfortable; self-indulgent

CONFUSED WORDS

M

macabre: gruesome
micawber: a baseless optimist; a spendthrift

made: v., past participle of to make
maid: n., a female servant

magnate: a powerful person in business
magnet: a metal object that attracts iron

mail: n., letters; v., to post
male: adj., masculine; n., a man

majority: more than half
plurality: largest number although less than half

mall: n., a shopping area
maul: v., to handle roughly

-mania: an abnormally intense enthusiasm for something
-philia: a tendency toward or abnormal attraction to
-phobia: an abnormal fear of something

manikin: a model of a human body with parts that detach
mannequin: a clothes dummy

manner: way
manor: an estate

manslaughter: see *homicide*

mantel: a wood or marble structure above a fireplace
mantle: a sleeveless cloak; region between the Earth's core and crust

margin: the difference between two figures
ratio: relation between two figures. If a committee votes 4–2, the margin is
    two votes and the ratio is 2-to-1.

marital: pertaining to marriage
marshal: v., to direct; n., title of an official in the military, police or fire depart-
    ment, or the person leading a parade
Marshall: n., the name
martial: adj., warlike; pertaining to the military, as in "martial law"

mask: n., a disguise; v., to disguise
masque: n., a masquerade, an amateur musical drama

masseur: man who gives massages
masseuse: woman who gives massages

masterful: powerful; fit to command
masterly: expert

material: thing out of which something is made
materiel: supplies of a military force

may, might: see *can, could*

may be: v., as in "it may be late"
maybe: adv.; perhaps

meat: the flesh of an animal
meet: v. to get together or be introduced; n., a gathering; adj., proper
mete: v., to distribute; n., a measure, a boundary

medal: an award
meddle: to interfere
metal: a class of elements including gold, iron, copper, etc.
mettle: character

media: plural. Example: "The media are wolves."
medium: singular. Example: "The medium is the message."

meretricious: deceptive; attracting attention in a gaudy way
meritorious: deserving merit

might: may; see *can, could*
mite: a small arachnid; a small object; a small amount

mil: measure of wire
mill: one-tenth of a cent

militate: to work against
mitigate: to lessen

miner: one who mines
minor: underage; lesser

minks: plural for the furry animal
minx: a mischievous girl

mislead: present tense
misled: past tense

misogamy: hatred of marriage
misogyny: hatred of women

mistake: see *error*

moat: a ditch filled with water for protection
mote: a speck, as of dust

mold: fungus; form
molt: to shed

momentary: short-lived
momentous: important

moot: open to argument
mute: speechless

moral: adj., virtuous; n., a lesson
morale: confidence or spirits of a person or group

more than: used with figures
over: usually spatial; however, AP allows such constructions as "He is over 40" or "I gave over $100." Probably best to use only in spatial sense to avoid confusion.

morning: n., early part of the day
mourning: n., adj., v., grieving

most: adj., greatest amount, degree or size
almost: adv., nearly

motif: a main theme or repeated figure
motive: inner drive

motor: see *engine*

mucous: adj., secreting mucus
mucus: n., liquid secreted

murder: see *homicide*

mutual: shared
reciprocal: interacting

N

nation: see *country*

nauseated: how you feel when your stomach turns
nauseous: what something is if it makes your stomach turn

naval: pertaining to the navy
navel: n., bellybutton, as in "navel orange"

negligent: careless
negligible: unimportant; small

neither: not either
nether: below

new: recent
novel: unusual

none: not any; not one
nun: a female member of a religious order

notable, noteworthy: worth noting
noted: famous
noticeable: capable of being seen; prominent
notoriety, notorious: having a bad reputation

O

oar: n., a long paddle
o'er: prep., over (poetic)
or: conj.

ore: n., mineral deposit

obsequies: funeral rites
obsequious: sickeningly respectful

observance: n., paying heed to a custom or ritual
observation: n., the act of viewing

obtuse: see *abstruse*

ocean: water between continents, the floor of which is made of dense basaltic rock
sea: narrower body of water than an ocean, the floor of which is made of lighter granitic rock of the continent

oculist: may be either an ophthalmologist or an optometrist
ophthalmologist: physician treating illnesses of the eyes
optician: makes eyeglasses (need not be a physician)
optometrist: measures vision (need not be a physician)

ode: n., a lyric poem
owed: v., past participle of to owe

odious: hateful
odorous: fragrant

official: authorized
officious: meddlesome

older, oldest: see *elder, eldest*

omnifarious: adj., of all kinds
omnivorous: eating any kind of food

one another: see *each other*

opaque: cannot be seen through
translucent: can be seen through but not clearly
transparent: can be clearly seen through

oral: see *aural*

ordinance: a law
ordnance: weapons and ammunition

other: adj. Example: "Turn the other cheek."
otherwise: adv. Example: "He's 50, but she thinks otherwise."

over: see *more than*

overdo: v., to do to excess
overdue: adj., tardy

P

packed: v., past participle of *to pack*
pact: n., an agreement

CONFUSED WORDS

paddy: a swamp
patty: a flat, usually fired, cake

pail: n., a bucket
pale: adj., light

pain: n., v., hurt
pane: n., sheet of glass

pained: receiving pain
painful: giving pain

pair: couple
pare: to trim
pear: n., the fruit

palate: roof of the mouth
palette: board on which paint is mixed
pallet: a small, hard bed; a small platform for moving and storing cargo; a tool for mixing clay; a tool for applying gold leaf

parameter: a constant used for determining the value of variables
perimeter: the curved, outer boundary of an area

pardon: to release a person from further punishment for a crime
parole: early release of someone imprisoned
probation: what one receives who is sentenced but not sent to jail

parity: equality
parody: a comic imitation

parlay: v., to increase
parley: v., to talk

part: a piece
portion: an allotment

partake of: to share
participate in: to take part in

partially: to a limited degree; in a biased way
partly: part of the whole

passed: v., past participle of to pass
past: n., history (see *last*)

patience: endurance
patients: people receiving treatment

pause: a break
paws: animal feet

peace: opposite of war; calm
piece: a part

peaceable: disposed to peace; promoting calm

154

peaceful: tranquil; not characterized by strife. Suspects surrender peacefully, not peaceably (unless they are antiwar demonstrators).

peak: n., a high point; v., to reach a high point
peek: n., a brief look; v., to look briefly
pique: n., a transient feeling of wounded vanity; v., to provoke

peal: to ring or resound
peel: to pare

pedal: a lever operated by the foot
peddle: to sell
petal: part of a flower

pediatrist: a children's doctor
podiatrist: a foot doctor

peer: an equal
pier: a platform extending from shore over water (see *dock*)

penal: pertaining to punishment
penile: pertaining to the penis

penance: an act of repentance
pennants: flags

pendant: n., an ornament worn around the neck
pendent: adj., hanging

penitence: feeling of remorse
penitents: people showing remorse

people: AP prefers this as the plural for *person* in all instances.
persons: Many usage experts argue that this should be used as the plural of *person* when an exact or small number of people is defined and that *people* should be used only to refer to large masses; AP prefers *people* for both meanings.

peremptory: decisive
pre-emptory: prior

perquisite: privilege
prerequisite: requirement

persecute: to oppress
prosecute: to take to court

personal: private; individual
personnel: employees; staff

perspective: view
prospective: expected

perspicacious: having great insight
perspicuous: easily understood

CONFUSED WORDS

persuade: see *convince*

petroglyph: a carving on stone
pictograph: a painting on stone

phenomena: plural
phenomenon: singular

physical: see *fiscal*

pidgin: a combination of languages
pigeon: the bird

pistil: part of a flower
pistol: a handgun

pitfall: a danger not easily anticipated
pratfall: a fall on the rump; a humilitating blunder

plain: n., flat country; adj., not fancy
plane: n., airplane, type of tool; v., to shave level

plaintiff: n., a person who sues
plaintive: adj., mournful

plurality: see *majority*

podium, dais: a platform to stand on while speaking
lectern: the stand behind which the speaker speaks

pole: a stick
poll: a survey; a voting place

pompon: an ornamental puff carried by cheerleaders
pom-pom: anti-aircraft fire

pomposity, pompousness: synonyms

polite: see *courteous*

poor: lacking
pore: n., opening in the skin; v., to study carefully
pour: v., to make a liquid flow

poplar: the tree
popular: well-liked

populous: full of people
populace: the common people

poring over: looking over
pouring over: emptying a liquid on

portend: v., to foreshadow
portent: n., an omen

practical: describes a sensible person or thing
practicable: describes a thing that's possible

pray: to worship
prey: n., a hunted animal; v., to plunder or hunt

precede: to go before
proceed: to continue

precipitant, precipitate: adj., rash
precipitous: steep

predominant: adj.
predominate: v.

premier: n., a prime minister; adj., outstanding
premiere: n., first presentation of a movie or play. Do not use as a verb or adjective, although many authorities permit it.

prescribe: to order
proscribe: to prohibit; to condemn

presence: act of being present; bearing
presents: gifts

presentiment: a premonition
presentment: a presentation

presumptive: founded on presumption
presumptuous: taking too many liberties

pretense: a false or unsupported claim of distinction
pretext: what is put forward to conceal the truth

primer: an elementary textbook; substance used to prepare a surface for painting
primmer: adj., more prim

principal: n., someone or something first in rank; adj., most important
principle: n., a basic rule or guide

prodigy: something or someone extraordinary
protege: someone guided or helped by someone more influential

profit: money made on a transaction
prophet: one who foresees

prohibit: see *forbid*

prone: lying face downward
supine: lying face upward

prophecy: noun
prophesy: verb

proposal: a plan offered for acceptance or rejection
proposition: an assertion set forth for argument

prostate: a male gland
prostrate: to lie prone

proved: past tense of prove
proven: adjective meaning tested and found effective

purposefully: aiming at a goal
purposely: intentionally
purposively: psychological term for opposite of aimlessly

Q

quarts: plural of quart, the measurement
quartz: the mineral

quash: to annul
squash: to crush

quaver: to tremble the voice
quiver: to shake

quell: to suppress
quench: to satisfy thirst; to douse

queue: see *cue*

quiet: silent
quite: very

R

rack: n., a stretching frame used for torture; v., to torture, to strain
reek: to give off a strong, bad odor
wrack: n., damage brought about by violence, as in "wrack and ruin"; best avoided as a verb
wreak: to inflict, as in "wreak havoc" or "wreak vengeance"
wreck: to damage or destroy

rain: precipitation
reign: term of a sovereign's power
reins: straps to control a horse; used in expression "free rein," meaning lossened control

raise: transitive (but bread raises); raise, raised, has raised
raze: v., to destroy
rise: intransitive; rise, rose, has risen

rare: in short supply all the time
scarce: in short supply temporarily

ravage: to destroy
ravish: to rape and carry away by force; to enrapture

real: adj. Example: "The clock is real."
really: adv. Example: "She is really tired."

reapportion: applies to state legislatures
redistrict: applies to congressional districts

rebound: to spring back
redound: to have a result

reciprocal: see *mutual*

recourse: a resort; that to which one turns for help
resource: a supply

re-cover: to cover again
recover: to regain health or possession

recur: to happen again often
reoccur: to happen again once

relaid: laid again
relayed: transmitted

reluctant: unwilling to act
reticent: unwilling to speak

remediable: capable of being fixed
remedial: intended as a remedy

rend: to split apart; to distress
render: to submit; to extract by melting

repairable: used with something physical that can be repaired
reparable: used with something not physical that can be repaired—such as a mistake

repel: to drive back
repellent: adj.; n., something that repels
repulse: v., to rebuff by discourtesy; to disgust
repulsive: adj., offensive; disgusting

replica: a copy made by the original artist or under that person's supervision
reproduction: a copy made by someone else

re-sign: to sign again
resign: to quit; to give up a job or office

respectable: worthy of respect
respectful: showing respect
respective: in order

resume: to start again
résumé: a summing up, especially of a career

review: a critical examination or scholarly journal
revue: a theatrical production with skits, music and dancing

right: correct
rite: a religious ceremony

wright: a worker
write: to put down in words

robbery: see *burglary*

role: an assumed part
roll: n., a kind of pastry; v., to tumble

round: a single shot
salvo: a succession of shots
volley: a number of simultaneous shots

rout: an overwhelming defeat resulting in confusion
route: a way traveled

rye: n., a kind of grass
wry: adj., twisted

S

sac: a pouch in a plant or animal
sack: bag for carrying goods

salary: a fixed compensation for a non-hourly worker
wages: pay to a worker

sanguine: ruddy; cheerful
sanguinary: bloody

saving: a bargain
savings: money in a bank

sculpture: see *figurine*

seasonable: suitable to the occasion
seasonal: occurring during a particular season

sensual: licentious
sensuous: pertaining to the senses

sentence: see *fine*

serf: a person in feudal servitude
surf: n., edge of the sea that breaks when it hits shore; v., to ride waves on a board

settler: one who settles down
settlor: one who makes a legal property settlement

sewage: human waste
sewerage: the system that carries away sewage

sex: see *gender*

shear: to shave; to cut
sheer: v., to swerve; adj., steep, transparent, thin

CONFUSED WORDS

since: see *because*

skew: v., to distort; to place at an angle
skewer: n., a long pin; v., to pierce with a skewer

slatternly: in the manner of a disorderly, unkempt woman
slovenly: in the manner of a disorderly, unkempt person

sleight: n., skill, especially at deceiving
slight: adj., meager; v., to neglect

sniffle: to sniff repeatedly
snivel: to whine

sociable: enjoying company
social: pertaining to society

solecism: a violation of grammar, usage or property
solipsism: belief that nothing is real but the self

solidarity: a show of support for
solidity: firm, stable

soluble: capable of being dissolved; capable of being solved
solvable: capable of being solved

spade: a shovel
spayed: had ovaries removed

specially: see *especially*

specie: coin
species: the biological term for a grouping more distinct than genus

specious: deceptive; used to describe abstract things
spurious: counterfeit; used to describe concrete things

stable: n., an animal shelter; adj., sturdy
staple: constantly used commodity

staid: sedate
stayed: past tense of stay

stanch: v., to restrain
staunch: adj., firm in opinion

stationary: adj., not moving
stationery: n., writing paper

statue: see *figurine*

stimulant: alcohol or drugs
stimulus: an incentive

straight: not crooked
strait: singular. Geographers prefer this term for a narrow passage connecting two bodies of water.

straits: plural. This term is accurate when there is more than one strait, as in the Straits of Mackinac.

successive: see *consecutive*

suit: n., a set of clothes; a lawsuit; v., to please
suite: n., a set of furniture, rooms or dance pieces

summon: v. Example: "Summon him to court."
summons: singular noun; Example "Give her a summons." Also, third-person singular verb.
summonses: plural noun; Example: "Give them summonses."

superficial: on or near the surface
superfluous: more than needed

sure: adj. Example: "He is sure to attend."
surely: adv. Example: "Surely she knows better."

systematic: systemlike
systemic: affecting the whole system

T

tack: a course of action
tact: ability to do the kind thing in a delicate situation

talesman: person summoned to fill a jury
talisman: a charm

taught: past tense of teach
taunt: to mock
taut: tight
tout: to praise; to solicit

team: a squad
teem: abound

tempera: painting
tempura: cooking

temporal: earthly
temporary: not permanent

tenant: person who lives in a rented house
tenet: a doctrine

terminable: able to be ended
terminal: at the end

theft: see *burglary*

therefor: for it, for that, for them
therefore: for that reason

think: see *feel*

thorough: complete
threw: past tense of "throw"
through: prep.; avoid "thru"

thrash: to beat an opponent. "To thrash something out" means to settle something with a detailed discussion.
thresh: to tramp grain

throne: a seat
thrown: past perfect of "throw"

tic: a twitch
tick: a bloodsucking arachnid

til: a sesame plant used in India for food and oil
'til: acceptable but not preferred shortened form of "until"
till: preferred shortened form of "until"; plow; money tray

tocsin: a disaster signal
toxin: a poisonous substance of animal or plant origin

toe: n., one of five on the foot
tow: v., to pull

tort: legal name for a wrongful act
torte: a kind of round, layer cake

tortuous: twisting; complex; deceitful
torturous: pertaining to torture

tread: to trample; present tense
trod: past tense

troop: a group of soldiers, police, highway patrol officers, scouts, people or animals
trope: a figure of speech
troupe: a company of actors, dancers or singers

trooper: a cavalry soldier, mounted police officer or highway patrol officer
trouper: a member of a theatrical company; a veteran performer

turbid: dense
turgid: bloated

U

under: see *fewer*

unexceptionable: beyond reproach
unexceptional: common

uninterested: see *disinterested*

unquestionable: indisputable
unquestioned: something that has not been questioned

V

vain: possessing vanity
vane: device for showing wind direction
vein: a blood vessel; a streak

valance: a short curtain
valence: an atom's capacity to combine

varmint: regional variation of "vermin"; plural: "varmints"
vermin: disease-carrying pest; plural: "vermin"

venal: corruptible
venial: minor
venerable: worthy of respect

veracious: truthful
voracious: tremendously hungry

verbal: see *aural, oral*

verbiage: excess words
wording: how something is said

vertex: highest point
vortex: a whirlpool

vial: n., a small bottle
vile: adj., evil
viol: n., a kind of stringed instrument

vice: corruption
vise: a tool for gripping

viral: pertaining to a virus
virile: having masculine strength

viscose: n., a solution used to make rayon
viscous: adj., sticky fluid

visible: able to be seen
visual: received through sight

W

waive: to give up or no longer require
waiver: the giving up of a claim
wave: n., a curve of something; v., to shake back and forth
waver: v., to falter

wangle: to get by contrivance
wrangle: to bicker

warranty: see *guarantee*

way: manner
weigh: v., to check for weight

weather: see *if*

wench: a serving girl; peasant girl; a wanton woman
winch: a machine used in hoisting

we're: contraction for "we are"
were: past tense of "to be"
where: adv.

wet: v., to moisten; adj., moist
whet: v., to sharpen, as in "whet your appetite"

wharf: see *dock*

whether: see *if*
whither: where
wither: to dry up

who's: contraction for "who is"
whose: possessive of "who"

wrack: see *rack*

Y

yoga: the religious and physical discipline
yogi: one who practices yoga

yoke: a device or symbol for subjugation
yolk: the yellow part of an egg

your: possessive of "you"
you're: contraction for "you are"

youth: boy or girl 13–18; singular
youths: plural

CONFUSED WORDS

Misused Words

Some words frequently are misused. Here is a list of common problems:

a (name): Don't say "There's a Jane Henderson here"—the *a* is unnecessary and insulting in that it diminishes a person's uniqueness; just say "Jane Henderson is here."

165

above: This preposition is often misused as an adjective. Correct usage: "The plane flew *above* the clouds." Incorrect: "The statement *above* should appear as a warning."

administer a blow: A blow is *dealt*, not *administered*.

affinity: This noun may be followed by the prepositions *between, of* or *with* but not *for*; however, *penchant for* is correct.

aghast: Use only if you mean paralysis of action.

ain't: Use *isn't*.

alas: Avoid this archaic word.

all: Don't say, for example, "Fife, Griffith and Smith were all released," but "Fife, Griffith and Smith were released."

all-important: An overblown and overused phrase, which means *everything*; depends on the word being modified; few things fit that description.

all-round: Not *all-around*. "Around" refers to position regarding a circle; "round" means full or complete.

allegedly: Never use; the word itself offers no legal protection and may actually get you into trouble. Instead, give the charge and identify the person making it.

and: Many books tell you not to begin a sentence with *and*. Some editors will let you, but most won't; they are more likely to let you begin a sentence with *but*.

annual: Don't say *first annual*—something isn't annual until the second time.

aren't I?: Use *am I not?*

as to: Do not use in place of *or* or *for; about* or *on* is preferable.

as yet: Wordy; change to *yet*.

awesome: Something evoking awe, an emotion of mingled reverence, wonder and dread; often misused for lesser feelings.

awful: An adjective; do not use in place of adverbs such as *very, really* or *extremely*.

backward: Note the lack of an *s* at the end.

bankrupt: Should not be used to describe a company reorganizing under bankruptcy laws. A person or company is bankrupt only if ordered by a court to liquidate assets.

belittle: Use to mean *disparage*, not merely *ridicule*.

bomb: It's not a bomb if it doesn't have an explosive charge; a tear-gas canister is, therefore, not a bomb.

bosom: A woman has a bosom, not bosoms, because the word means a human, usually female, chest.

centers around: Use *centers on* or *revolves around* because the center is the middle of a circle—the point around which things circle.

city: An area isn't a city unless incorporated.

cohort: Unless you're trying to be funny, don't use to mean colleague.

commandeer: Use to mean *to seize something for use by the government, especially the military*. Using it merely to mean *to take something by force* is colloquial; using it to mean *take charge of* is incorrect.

condone: Use to mean *excuse, forgive, pardon, overlook*; do not use to mean *accept, approve, certify, endorse, sanction*.

controversial: Wilson Follett believes incorrectly that the word originally meant *engaging in controversy*, not merely *disputed*; consequently, he argues that it should not be used in the second sense, though a check with the Oxford English Dictionary shows that he has the history backward. Better yet, don't use this buzzword at all—instead, *show* why the person or thing is controversial rather than merely labeling it so.

crescendo: Because a crescendo is a gradual rise in sound volume or intensity, it is redundant to write *rose to a crescendo*.

decimate: The word, originally meaning to *kill every tenth person*, has come to mean *destroy*, and most authorities now find that acceptable.

déjà vu: Use to refer only to the *illusion* that something has been experienced before; if it actually was experienced, the feeling isn't *deja vu*.

depart: *Depart* always should be followed by *from* except in the phrase *depart this life*.

devalued: Not *devaluated*.

diagnose: Doctors *diagnose* a patient's *condition*, not the patient.

dialogue: William Safire says that though many insist the word be used only as a noun to mean *conversation between two people*, it may also be used as a verb and to mean *a conversation among more than two*: The word is derived from the Greek *dia* meaning across, not from *di* meaning two, he points out; the use of the word as a verb is not a recent invention but dates back to 1597.

different from: The AP Stylebook says never to write *different than*, so know that most editors will insist on that. H.W. Fowler says that such a rule, however, is a superstition, and the Oxford English Dictionary lists uses of the phrases *different than* by Addison and Steele, Defoe, Coleridge and Thackeray. The Washington Post Deskbook probably is correct when it says either is correct but *different from* is preferred.

dilemma: Often misused to mean merely an unpleasant situation or a quandary, the word means *a choice between two* (and only two) *bad alternatives*, although it can also mean (but rarely does) *a hard choice between two good alternatives*; it should not be used to mean *a choice between a good alternative and a bad one*. Also note that there is no *n* in dilemma, contrary to many people's misperceptions.

epitome: Not merely a high point, an epitome is the ideal embodiment of something.

erstwhile: Means *former*, not *earnest*.

estimate: Because an estimate is an approximation, it is redundant to follow it with *about*; so, instead of writing that a crowd was *"estimated at about 500,"* write that it was *"estimated at 500."*

exploded: Avoid the hyperbolic expression that someone "exploded" when what you mean is that he or she became angry.

fail: Because this means to be unsuccessful at something, a pitcher, for example, cannot fail to strike out a batter—unless he was trying to.

famed: Shakespeare and Dryden used it in place of *famous*, but most editors reject it because they think it's journalese.

fire: A legally dangerous word too often used loosely, *fired* should not be used to describe someone who was laid off or quit.

following: Don't use as a preposition; change to *after*.

forbid to: Forbid takes *to*; prohibit takes *from*.

forward: Note the lack of an *s* on the end.

gay: Theodore Bernstein and other editors have complained about the use of the word to mean homosexual, but Chaucer used it as early as the 14th century to refer to a loose woman, so it's long had a sexual connotation. A 19th-century dictionary of slang defined the word as meaning dissipated or "given to the use of men." The AP Stylebook permits *gay* as an adjective but not as a noun.

genius: Avoid this overused noun.

half a: Not *a half*

hey: Avoid what Joseph Epstein calls "the California Hey"—*hey* inserted needlessly in a sentence.

hike: Do not use as a verb to mean *increase*.

holocaust: A bad fire or accident is not a holocaust unless many people are killed or there is great destruction. Have enough respect for the Holocaust in World War II not to use this word lightly.

imbecile: The word is the same as an adjective or a noun; do not use *imbecilic*.

into (something): Avoid this 1960s expression; instead write *interested in*.

intriguing: Do not use as a synonym for *fascinating*.

legendary: An overused adjective.

like: Like is a preposition that introduces phrases and should not be used as a conjunction introducing clauses; do not confuse it with *as* ("Winston tastes good, *as* a cigarette should."), *as if* or *as though* ("Act *as if*—or *as though*—you mean it.") or *that* ("I feel *that* I should be doing something.").

livid: Use to mean *furious* or *black and blue*; it is often misused to mean *vivid* or *red*.

momentarily: Like the adjective *momentary*, this adverb means *lasting only a moment*; some usage guides suggest it should not be used to mean *in a moment*, although most consider that acceptable.

mutual: Because it applies to a relationship between two, this adjective should not be used in the broader sense to mean *shared* or *common*, which may refer to a relationship among more than two.

nab: Use to mean *grab, steal* or *snatch*; don't use if something was earned.

nohow: There is no such word; say *anyway*.

nor: Some people use *nor* instead of *or* after any negative expression, but most grammarians say this is an overcorrection.

O, Oh: *O* is not followed by a comma and is used in addressing someone: "O Father, I have something to tell you''; *Oh* is followed by a comma or an exclamation point and is used for exclamation rather than address.

obsolete: Do not use this adjective as a verb.

ongoing: This omnipresent adjective actually says nothing because use of a present-tense verb alone means "still in existence.'' As William Zinsser points out, "When we cease to be ongoing we are dead.''

other: Required in comparisons of the same class: "My Ford breaks down more than any other car I've owned''; otherwise omit.

overly: Don't use. *Over* is already an adverb and should be used instead; so, say someone is "overqualified'' not "overly qualified.''

own: Often redundant, as in "do your own thing.''

personable: This adjective means *shapely* or *attractive*; it shouldn't be used to mean having a pleasing personality.

pivotal: Use to mean *crucial*, not merely *important*. A crucial vote is not an important election, but rather a vote on which an election depends.

police: Need not be preceded by "the.''

poorly: Do not use for *bad*.

practically: This adverb means *for all practical purposes*; it should not be used to mean *almost*.

presently: Despite widespread use to mean *now*, many editors prefer using it only to mean *soon*.

prevaricate: Use to mean *to evade the truth or stray from it*, not necessarily *to lie*. For example, an equivocation is prevarication because it misleads, even though the statement may be literally true.

prohibit from: Prohibit takes *from*; forbid takes *to*.

quite: Avoid whenever possible. The word means *entirely* or *all the way* and should not be used to mean *considerably*, *rather* or *somewhat*. It should never be followed by a noun.

reaction: Don't use in place of *opinion*.

refute: Use to mean to disprove, not merely dispute or rebut.

reportedly: Avoid; an excuse for laziness about looking up the facts and a way to try to avoid responsibility for a statement.

reverend: This adjective always takes the article *the* in front of it; someone should never be called *a reverend*, because as former Episcopal priest

MISUSED WORDS

169

Alan Watts points out in his autobiography, the word is an adjective, not a noun.

safari: Use to mean a hunting expedition, not merely a trip.

similar to: Not similar *with*.

some: Do not substitute this adjective for the adverbs *rather* or *somewhat*.

sometime: Use to mean *former*, not *occasional*.

strikebreaker: Use to mean someone hired to take the place of a striker, not just anyone who crosses a picket line such as a manager or a union member who decides to work anyway.

superior to: Not superior *than*.

temperatures: Described as *higher* or *lower* but not as *warmer* or *cooler*.

terrified: More than simply scared, *terrified* means paralyzed by fear.

that: The AP Stylebook says journalists should use *that* following these verbs: *to advocate, to assert, to contend, to declare, to estimate, to make clear, to point out, to propose* and *to state*. Use *that* rather than *as* after the verbs *to feel, to say* or *to think*; other books add *to feel, to know, to say* and *to think* to that list.

thus: Change this conjunctive adverb to *so*, which is less pompous.

too: Do not use to begin a sentence; instead use *Also*. Do not use as a synonym for *very*. *Too* should be set off by commas, and when used with a past participle, it requires an intervening word such as *highly, little, much, greatly*.

toward: Note the lack of an *s* on the end.

transpire: Use to mean *to leak out* or *to become known*, not merely *to happen*.

trek: Don't use as a synonym for trip or journey; a *trek* is a slow journey filled with hardships.

under way: Generally used as two words. *Underway* is correct only in nautical use before a noun, as in *underway convoy*. Better, use *started* or *began*.

unthawed: There is no such adjective; use *frozen*.

up: Do not use as a verb.

very: Cut whenever possible; if you use it with a past participle, it requires an intervening word such as *greatly, highly, little, much*.

viewpoint: *Point of view* is better.

virtually: Use to mean *in effect, though not in fact*; in most cases, *almost* or *nearly* is better.

when: Do not use to mean *by the time that*; for example, rewrite "Most of the house was destroyed when firefighters arrived" as "Most of the house was destroyed by the time firefighters arrived". Also, clauses introduced by an adverb should not be used in place of a noun or pronoun: "Sinning is *when you separate yourself from God*. Rewrite as a noun phrase: Sinning is *the act of separating yourself from God*.

where: Do not use for *that*: "I saw on the news *that* the vice president is coming to town."

while: Some experts say that *while* should be used only to mean *simultaneously*, not in place of *and, but, though* or *although*. If it's the first word in a sentence and it's meant to show contrast, change it to *although*; if it's meant to show contrast later in the sentence, use *though* or *but*.

whose: This possessive pronoun should only be used with people or animals. *Wrong*: "The door *whose* lock was broken, had to be replaced." *Right*: "The door, the lock *of which* was broken, had to be replaced."

worse: Do not use to mean *more*.

worst way: Do not use to mean *very much*.

yet: Some say this word should always have a comma after it, but we would just say *consider* using a comma—we've seen plenty of places where we wouldn't put one.

zoom: This word refers only to upward motion. Do not say, for example, that someone zoomed down the highway.

MISUSED WORDS

CHAPTER 9

Sexism, Racism and Other "-isms"

by Jean Gaddy Wilson

In the late 20th century we are faced with a culture that is changing and a language that has trouble catching up.

That makes writers' roles pivotal. Journalists are supposed to send out messages that reflect current reality, not assumptions from earlier and less-inclusive ages. Yet in our use of the language we often rely on time-worn stereotypes that fail to reflect those new realities.

Using words to convey the reality brought about by the 1960s civil rights and women's movements means tampering with accepted patterns of the past. Many of the spelling, grammar and punctuation rules covered earlier in this book evolved from Latin, a language that is dead. Many of the concepts discussed in this chapter evolved during the past three decades. The question, then, is how a language grounded in Latin copes with such change.

The answer is that Latin may be dead, but English isn't. Like all living languages, English constantly evolves and changes to fit new realities. In the E.B. White and William Strunk Jr. classic, The Elements of Style, it's clearly stated:

> The language is perpetually in flux: It is a living stream, shifting, changing, receiving new strength from a thousand tributaries, losing old forms in the backwaters of time.

Rules derived from Latin differentiated nouns by feminine and masculine gender, such as using the suffix -trix to signify female form of executive, executrix. Those rules may still apply in legal language but don't fit the rest of today's world. Imagine Fortune magazine referring to Katharine Graham, chief executive officer of the Washington Post Co. and the only woman to head one of the 500 top corporations in the United States, as an executrix.

Our goal should be to provide an inclusive, non-biased and non-judgmental language that reflects today's reality. By eliminating both blatant and subtle sexism, racism, ageism and other stereotypes from our writing and speech, we actually provide a more reliable, credible look at today's culture.

To understand what's appropriate in today's language, it's important to look backward.

A BRIEF HISTORY OF -ISMs

We live in a society that for centuries has treated women and minorities as peripheral. A language that displays a bias against women and minorities reflects that history of inequality.

When the Pilgrims settled here, they brought English common law with them. When "Blackstone's Commentaries on the Laws of England" was imported to this country as the basis of our legal system, women and children (particularly female children) were legally on a par with the master's cattle, oxen and dogs. And when slavery was institutionalized into the country's laws, black women and men were given the same legal status accorded white women and children. All were property belonging to white men.

Black men gained citizenship when they got the vote after the Civil War in the 1860s. White and black women were elevated to citizen level when they won the vote in 1920. But minorities and females of all races began to gain equal access to employment, credit and education only in the mid-1960s.

Documents serving as the foundation of this country's government held white males in higher value: "We hold these truths to be self-evident; that all men are created equal."

For those who would argue that "men" was generic then or now and included or includes everyone, remember that two constitutional amendments were required to bring adults other than white males into the voting process. So, what we're faced with in today's usage is centuries of authoritative language diminishing the roles of women and minorities.

But society changes. The social revolutions of the mid-1960s were and are partly about renaming what is. Language must catch up to a world in which the poor, the disabled, women, blacks, Asian Americans, Native Americans, Hispanics, Latinos and Chicanos are given full credit for being citizens on a peer level with average white men.

WHAT TO AVOID

To better reflect reality in the world today, we should avoid the following "-isms" both in specific words and in areas of coverage.

Sexism

Sexism is usually thought of as set expectations about women's appearance, actions, skills, emotions and proper place in society. But sexism also includes sex-stereotyping of men.

Instead of myriad portrayals of individual women, five common stereotypes of females seem to emerge in news coverage, and they cloud today's reality. In most cases, these stereotypes are to be avoided.

1. *Mother/nurturer*—woman as caregiver. Examples: grand-mother, prostitute with a heart of gold, fairy godmother.

2. *Ugly stepmother/bitch*—woman as non-nurturer. Examples: Iron Maiden, aggressive woman, aloof executive.

3. *Pet/cheerleader*—woman as appendage to a man or children. Examples: first lady, the little lady, June Cleaver.

4. *Tempter/seducer*—woman as sexpot (a term used only for women). Examples: soap opera antagonist, gold digger, victim of sex crimes who "asked for it."

5. *Victim*—woman as incompetent. Examples: damsel in distress, helpless female.

Many times sexist writing is not immediately apparent. For example, in this UPI story, all women in public life are suggested as seducers:

> Gary Hart's fall from grace because of reports of womanizing has prompted politicians to examine their professional relationships with women, a Hart supporter said Sunday.
>
> "The sense on the floor of the Congress this week is that all rules have changed and all bets are off, that relationships are going to be changed for better or for worse, and people, sadly I think, are going to hesitate in their professional relationships with women on their staffs, women who work on their campaigns," said Rep. Robert Torricelli, D-N.J.

"There's going to be a caution that is not good for getting women involved in public life."

Men don't escape sex-role stereotyping either. Two major stereotypes for men emerge in language and should also be avoided:

1. *Macho man/Rambo*—man as battler. Examples: corporate raider, political strongman (no parallel word exists for women), master criminal, conquering hero.
2. *Wimp/enlightened man*—man as sensitive. Examples: Mama's boy, househusband, "faggot," caregiver, sissy.

Racism

Racism is discrimination against ethnic or racial groups based on the notion that one's own ethnic stock is superior; individual blacks, whites, Asian Americans, Native Americans, people of Spanish ancestry and any other races may be racist.

These are common stereotypes to be avoided:

1. *The secondary*—people of little consequence who serve the powerful. Examples: domestic help, migrant farmers, sweatshop workers.
2. *The ignored/the invisible*—people whose achievements are trivialized. Examples: Rico Tubbs' character (black) compared to Sonny Crockett's (white) on television's "Miami Vice," Jesse Jackson's being discounted as "unelectable," slum or reservation residents, the underclass.
3. *Achievers*—exceptions to the "norm." Examples: model minority, credit to one's race.
4. *The despised/feared*—outsiders, criminals, suspects. Examples: welfare cheats, illegal aliens, drug addicts, "animals."

The overall discounting of racial groups is apparent in this AP story, pointed out by Paula LaRocque, writing coach at The Dallas Morning News (later in the article it becomes clear that minorities means minority *males*):

Washington—whose local industry, the federal government, overregulates everything—has virtually no entry requirements

for would-be cabbies. Nine of 10 District cabs are owner-oper-
ated. In consequence, Washington has probably the nation's
best taxi service, as well as some splendid opportunities for minorities, who need scrape together only a car and a $25 license.

The invisibility of racial groups is perhaps most vividly apparent in accounts of an event that were corrected decades after the
fact: For generations, history books noted that the only survivor of
Custer's Last Stand at Little Big Horn was a horse, Comanche.
More than a century after the battle, in the 1960s, demonstrating
students at the University of Kansas (where the stuffed Comanche
was displayed in a glass case) pointed out that several thousand
Sioux also survived that day.

When minorities are made visible, the reference is sometimes
gratuitous and fosters old stereotypes: *Police in Kansas City are
searching today for a black man in his 30s who is suspected of
taking part in a 7-Eleven robbery late last night.*

How many black men in their 30s live in Kansas City? The
report is not a description. If height, weight and distinguishing
characteristics such as scars, speech patterns, etc., were used,
then enough information would have been given on which to base
an identification. The gratuitous addition of "black" simply adds a
label.

Ageism

Ageism is discrimination based on age, especially discrimination against middle-aged and elderly people.

In a youth-oriented culture, age is an issue for both men and
women. But the focus on age is usually not necessary and gets in
the way of the greater reality, as in these examples:

The spry 65-year-old salesman works five days a week in the job he's loved
for the past 30 years. (The story later says he founded the company.)

Grandmother Wins Election as Centralia Mayor (headline)

In the first example, *spry* gives the impression that the salesman is unusually active for his age. The assumption is unfair and
ageist. In the second example, *grandmother* is both ageist (it
focuses unduly on age) and sexist (it focuses on a woman's tie to

her family rather than an appropriate accomplishment—being elected mayor). Imagine this headline: *Grandfather Wins Election as Centralia Mayor.* That's one you're unlikely to see.

Other forms of stereotyping

Stereotyping denies the individuality of people or groups by expecting them to conform to unvarying patterns. An example:

> Jones said that after a woman who identified herself only as a "Jewish mother" complained that she and several co-workers were upset because of the lack of day care, the company began making plans to survey employees.

Even when a source uses a stereotype, such as *Jewish mother*, it is not the journalist's job to perpetuate that stereotype. In this example, it would be a simple matter to drop the offensive labeling. It's hard to imagine that the label is in any way necessary to the story.

Such labeling makes it easy for the narrow-minded to engage in discrimination. Perpetuating sexism, racism, ageism and other forms of stereotyping in the language helps contribute to such discrimination against individuals and groups.

No matter how unintentional, sexist, racist and ageist labels that creep into writing are not only unfair to groups and individuals; but also are inaccurate. A journalist's job is to reflect reality.

THE NON-BIAS RULE

The history of inequality in Western culture has led to a language that stresses white men as the standard and considers others as substandard.

Following one simple rule of writing or speaking will eliminate most biases. Ask yourself: Would you say the same thing about an affluent, white man?

The expectation is that white men are leaders and that leaders who are not white, able-bodied men are aberrations. Yet the reality is that women, minorities, disabled people and people older than 70 are leaders in communities, corporations and the nation.

Media coverage often slips into treating these leaders as less than able. For instance, when a male television talk show host interviewed Dorcas R. Hardy, commissioner of Social Security, about changes in that behemoth institution, he concluded the interview by saying:

> "You're the first woman and the youngest person to head this institution. Don't you feel overwhelmed?"

Is it pertinent that she is the first woman and youngest? Perhaps, although the constant stress on "first women" in stories says, "This person is unlike all others of her sex." The question implies that she may not be up to such an important job. The value of the official's work was trivialized by the interviewer as he focused on her sex, rather than on what she does.

One cannot imagine a black man being asked:

> "You're the first black and the youngest person ever to head this institution. Don't you feel overwhelmed?"

Nor would a white man have been asked:

> "You're the first white man and the youngest person ever to head this institution. Don't you feel overwhelmed?"

The point is that neither man's ability would have been questioned based on sex. Nor should a woman's.

Often, reporters treat men and women unequally, patronizing women by describing them or their dress when the same would not be done to a man. For example: "*The attractive, 35-year-old mother of three wore an all-business suit on her first day as managing editor.*" Would anyone have written: "*The handsome, 38-year-old father of three wore an all-business suit on his first day as managing editor*"?

Other non-equal media treatment is evident when members of minority groups are labeled by race. For example: "*Black poet Maya Angelou spoke to 500 persons about her new book.*" Would anyone have written: "*White poet Tom McAfee is memorialized in one of his student's poems*"?

Apply the non-bias rule to test whether your writing is even-handed and fair.

SYMBOLIC ANNIHILATION

A deeper problem for all groups, other than white men, is one of invisibility. Media messages show us who we are through language, a system of symbols that describe our existence, actions and opportunities. As both George Gerbner and Gaye Tuchman, sociologists who independently study the media, point out: If a group is not represented in media messages and the language, that group is not part of the picture we carry around in our heads. When a group is invisible, absent, condemned, trivialized or ignored in writing, people in that group are symbolically "zapped" from existence.

Sources for stories are "mainly male, mainly pale." Women and people from all ethnic and racial minorities are largely excluded from the realms of experts queried by the media. To give Americans a more realistic look at themselves, multicultural sources should be quoted.

Primarily because of the invisibility of women and racial minorities in the language, the achievements of white men are given more credence than those of a minority man or any woman. And though white men have always been presidents of the country, chiefs of the FBI and heads of the Armed Forces, it is unrealistic today to assume that the sex, age, race and physical abilities a person holds will neatly fit that person into old stereotypical boxes.

Many blacks are in the middle class, which runs counter to language placing blacks in poverty. More than half the women in the country are employed outside the home, which runs counter to the old image of women as housewives. Mentally retarded people are no longer shut away from participating in the world and their own lives. Disabled people may be no more handicapped than the "temporarily abled." Native Americans are not of one tribe. Americans of Spanish-speaking ancestry are not in a monolithic group; they are Cuban Americans, Mexican Americans, Puerto Rican Americans and others whose roots are in Spain, Latin America and Spanish-speaking Caribbean nations, all with differing cultural backgrounds. Asian-American students are not all stereotypically at the head of the class, nor are they of a monolithic group. Nor are Asian Americans of one monolithic group; they may be of Japanese, Chinese, Korean, Vietnamese, Thai or other ancestry.

The judgments of yesterday and today that ignore the individuality of people do not fit today's writing.

179

AVOIDING SEXIST REPORTING

Sexist premises that lead to non-reality reporting

By looking at common misperceptions of women, we can see how individuality in all groups may be masked.

Jean Ward, professor at the University of Minnesota, set out a "journalist's guide to sexist presumptions" in the late 1970s that shows how the individuality of women was denied them in news accounts.

By seeing these patterns, which have not changed substantially in the past decade, we can begin to understand how individuality in all groups may be denied. (Reprinted by permission from *Columbia Journalism Review*, May/June 1980.)

A. All people are male unless proven female.

- The "documentary" delightfully explores the rivalries between different orchestral sections, as well as some of the personal ones, like the feud between a woman cellist who takes nips from a whiskey bottle and a violinist she accuses of molesting little girls. (*The Minneapolis Tribune*, 11/14/79)

- San Francisco inducted its first group of homosexuals into the Police Department Tuesday. Nine women and 16 minority race recruits also were in the class of 50 cadets. (UPI, 11/14/79)

- LONDON—Legal history was made when a man was granted a high court order restraining a woman neighbor from enticing away his dog, a Pharaoh hound called Kinky. (*Los Angeles Times*, 8/30/79)

- (Regarding a bill regulating marital conduct:) Parliament, by an overwhelming majority, shelved the bill for six months. For the time being, therefore, Kenyans may continue to slap as many wives as they can afford. (*Time*, 8/6/79)

- Headline: "Woman Photographer Wins Smith Sabbatical" (*The Minneapolis Tribune*, 5/9/79)

- In fact, though no one ever talks about it very much, booze has played as big a part in the lives of modern American writers as talent, money, women and the longing to be top dog. (*Commentary*, 3/76)

B. A women's relationship to a man (or men) is her defining identity.

- The death penalty will be sought against a 24-year-old South Side man who pleaded guilty Tuesday to kidnapping, raping and murdering a doctor's wife last year, prosecutors said. (*Chicago Tribune*, 10/10/79)

- Hernando Williams stunned a Criminal Court room Tuesday by pleading guilty to the 1978 abduction and murder of Linda Goldstone, the wife of a North Side doctor. (*Chicago Sun-Times*, 10/10/79)

- Headline: "Death Ends Spinster's Fight Against Amputation" (*The Minneapolis Star*, 5/2/78)

C. A woman's appearance always requires comment, whether she defies or exemplifies a popular stereotype.

- At 38, she is still a stunner, with a robust sense of humor, a throaty, husky laugh and green eyes that sparkle like gemstones. (AP, 10/10/79)

- Thatcher—"Maggie" to her friends and to Fleet Street, "Mrs. T" to politicians outside her inner circle, and "the Blessed Margaret" to the Conservatives' resident wit, Norman St. John-Stevas—is a small, fine-boned woman, with pale blue eyes, the kind of complexion the English always liken to a rose and hair that she readily admits to dyeing blond. (*The New York Times*, 4/29/79)

D. A woman can safely be identified as "his wife"; it is unnecessary to identify her by name.

- Mundal, Norway—On a summer's day in 1956, a farmer named Fredrik Mundal, his wife and their 6-year-old son, Ole, set out on a long and perilous journey from this remote village of 400 people, nestled beneath the mighty Jostedalsbre glacier along the spectacular Fjaerlands Fjord. (*The New York Times*, 4/16/79)

E. Although stylebooks prohibit words with grafted feminine endings and such designations as "coed," ignore the rule if it suits you.

- Headline: "Re-entering College: Older Women Battle to Become Coeds Again" (*Los Angeles Times*, 9/9/79)

F. After marriage, a man remains a man and a woman becomes a wife.

- An Illinois man and wife were charged here Tuesday with illegal possession and intent to sell about 12 pounds of hashish worth about $30,000. (AP, 10/11/79)

G. Homemaking and parenting are not work.

- The Etelsons were married in 1950, and for the first years of their marriage, Mrs. Etelson operated a cafeteria in an industrial plant. She stopped working between 1958 and 1961 to care for her two young daughters. (*The Wall Street Journal*, 5/4/78)

181

H. It is newsworthy when a church member, parent and neighbor is successful in business or the professions, provided the successful person is a woman.

- To her neighbors in the Baltimore suburb of Towson, Md., Jean M. Kirk is simply a pleasant, church-going, working housewife and mother of four. But then there's the T. Rowe Price Associates Inc. business card that carries the title of assistant vice president. (*The Wall Street Journal*, 11/13/79)

I. Status as housewife takes precedence over all other kinds of status.

- For most farmers, a wife is an immense asset as a livestock feeder, errand-runner and extra tractor-driver. But Mr. Nelson's wife, Leona, is more than that; she ran the farm single-handedly five days a week for 20 years. (*The Wall Street Journal*, 5/22/79)

J. Events in a woman's life must be identified as A.M. (Ante Marriage) or P.M. (Post Marriage).

- Patricia Hearst Shaw, the newspaper heiress and pardoned bank robber, appeared Thursday with women's rights activist Gloria Allred at a Los Angeles news conference on battered women—one of her first public appearances since her marriage April 1. Ms. Hearst—who says she prefers using her maiden name—was kidnapped by the Symbionese Liberation Army in 1974 and convicted of participating in a bank robbery with SLA members. (*Los Angeles Times*, 9/9/79)

Other presumptions that exist are:

A woman's marital status takes precedence over all other factors in her life.

When Geraldine Ferraro was named the Democratic Party's vice presidential candidate in 1984, she continued using her given name professionally just as she had throughout her life. During the campaign and beyond, however, various members of the media (including *The New York Times*) only allowed the honorifics "Miss" and "Mrs." to be used when referring to a woman. The candidate, faced with two inaccurate choices, was forced to choose either "Miss" or "Mrs.," both of which were factually incorrect.

Mrs. would have been correct only if she had taken her husband's name. Then, she would have been Mrs. Geraldine Zaccaro.

Why was the error, "Mrs. Geraldine Ferraro," continued month after month? Because some members of the media at that point identified women by one of two courtesy titles, *Miss* or *Mrs.*, both predicated upon marriage or the lack of it.

Neither honorific fit the candidate's name (or other women who chose to marry but retain the names given them at birth).

The papers could have used *Ms.*, a title for women that is not tied to marriage and that dates back to the 1940s as a title analogous to *Mr.* Also, *Ms.* was adopted by The Associated Press in 1977 as an appropriate appellation. The *New York Times* began using *Ms.* on June 19, 1986.

Appearance is the primary attribute by which to measure a woman's worth.

In discussing high school teen-age suicides, a minister was quoted as saying:

> "One pretty little girl—she was so attractive—who made good grades, went into the school's bathroom and shot herself in the stomach. She had everything to live for. She was so attractive. Why would she do that?"

Would her attempted suicide have made more sense if she were ugly? Note two other sex-linked descriptors: *Pretty* and *little*. Diminutives are used to describe women, not men. Would a teen-age boy have been labeled "a pretty little boy?"

All professionals are male unless otherwise stipulated.

Some examples taken from newspapers:

The female attorney won the case.

The woman photographer won the award.

A female doctor was at the accident.

In all these examples, the sense of fairness expected from the media is assailed, and credibility is lost.

Eliminating sexist terminology

The word *man* does not include everyone. Although centuries of prior stress on *man* lingers, the term is exclusive and means, literally, "men."

As Casey Miller and Kate Swift make clear in the second edition of "The Handbook of Nonsexist Writing for Writers, Editors and Speakers," conventional English that uses generic masculine-gender words often "obscures the actions, the contributions and sometimes the very presence of women."

For example, to credit the habitation and civilization of the world to "man" leaves out all women. Of course, without women there would be no children, hence no habitation. The use of the generic "man" (*Pilgrim Fathers, forefathers*, etc.) obscures reality.

Making language inclusive is fairly simple:

Use *man* only when referring to a man or a group of men. When a word describes a group that includes women and men, or could include men and women, no matter how few of either sex, use a gender-free word. When a word describes an individual, it's still preferable to use a gender-free word. If you feel you must tie the descriptor to one sex, remember that almost any word ending with the suffix *-man* can end with the suffix *-woman*.

Here are some ways to avoid confusion:

advertising representative—not *adman*
all people are created equal—not *all men are created equal*
anchor—for all those anchoring the news, or specifically *anchorwoman* for a woman anchoring the news, *anchorman* for a man anchoring the news
artisan—not *craftsman*
assembly member—for all elected to the assembly (or *assemblywoman* or *assemblyman*)
brotherly and sisterly love—not *brotherly love*
business professional or *executive*—for all those in business (or *businessman* or *businesswoman*)
camera operator—for all persons operating video cameras
chairperson, convener, presider, coordinator—for all those chairing meetings (or specifically *chairwoman* or *chairman*). The AP Stylebook still requires the gender-linked *chairwoman/chairman*, using *chairperson* only if the word is an organization's formal title for an office; however, *chairperson* has become common in spoken language.
common person, average person—not *common man, average man*
congressional representative—for members of Congress (or *congressman* or *congresswoman*)

councilor—for member of the council (or *councilwoman* or *councilman*)

door attendant—not *doorman*

deliverer or *delivery person*—not *delivery man*

drafter—not *draftsman*

every person for himself or herself—not *every man for himself*

English—not *Englishmen*

factory worker—not *factory man*

fisher—not *fisherman*

foreman, forewoman—not *foreman* for both sexes

French—not *Frenchmen*

Irish—not *Irishmen*

insurance representative—not *insurance man*

handmade or *synthetic*—not *manmade*; also use *manufactured, constructed, fabricated, created*

hotel attendant—not *bellman*

house worker—not *maid*

humanity, humankind—not *mankind*

husband and wife—not *man and wife*. Also, *wife and husband, man and woman, woman and man*

laity, laypeople, lay person—for members of the congregation as distinguished from clergy (or *layman* or *laywoman*)

line repairer—not *lineman*

meter reader—not *meter man* or *meter maid*

news carrier—not *news boy* or *news girl*

operate—not *man*, i.e., *operate the office* rather than *man the office*; also use *work, staff, serve*

operational space flight, carrying female and male astronauts—not *manned space flight*

people at work—not *men at work*

person-on-the-street interview—not *man-on-the-street interview*

personnel—not *manpower*; also use *staff, work force, workers*

police officer—for all members of a police department (or, specifically, *policewoman, policeman*)

postal worker—not *postman*; also use *mail carrier*

sales representative or *salesperson*—not *salesman* as generic (or, specifically, *saleswoman, salesman*)

spokesperson—or *representative* (or, specifically, *spokesman, spokeswoman*). The AP Stylebook still requires the gender-linked *spokeswoman/spokesman*; however, *spokesperson* is common in spoken language.

telephone worker—not *telephone man*

trades worker—not *tradesman*
utility-hole cover—not *manhole cover*
worker—not *working man*
worker's compensation—not *workman's compensation* (44 percent of the work force is female)

Feminine endings

The male-female suffixes for nouns often are unnecessary and are gradually disappearing from the language, especially the *-ess* ending for women.

The word *poetess*, for example, would not be used to describe Emily Dickinson or Sylvia Plath; the term is considered demeaning.

Similarly, the tendency is to use the generic *flight attendant* rather than the gender-specific *stewardess* or *steward*. In the acting community, the word *actor* has almost replaced the word *actress* in referring to women, except at the Academy Awards. And there is a growing trend to use the words *waiter* or *server* for both men and women, replacing the word *waitress* even in the singular. Here are some other examples:

author—not *author* (male) and *authoress* (female)
alumnae and *alumni*—not *alumni* alone for a group of men
   and women who have attended a school. Specifically,
   alumna (plural *alumnae*) is correct for woman (women);
   alumnus (plural alumni) for man (men). Your editor, backed
   by The AP Stylebook, will tell you *alumni* is the correct term
   for the group of men and women. However, just as *man* does
   not stand for all men and women, *alumni* does not stand for
   women and men who attended a school.
aviator—not *aviator* (male) and *aviatrix* (female)
birth name, given name—not *maiden name*
blond—In the interest of simplicity, the French *blonde* (female)
   and *blond* (male) could become genderless.
brunet—Again, the French *brunette* (female) and *brunet* (male)
   could become genderless.
coed—Don't use; this trivializes women and defines them as od-
   dities; use *student*.
divorce—Drop the French *divorcee* (female) to *divorce* (male).
   Extra care is necessary to use this term equally for men and
   women rather than focusing on women's marital status. Bet-

186

ter yet, if marital status is relevant, just say the person *is divorced.*

fiance—The French ending, tied to gender, can be dropped, rather than *fiance* (male) and *fiancee* (female). As with *divorce*, extra care is necessary so that women's marital status is not the focus.

hero—not *hero* (male) and *heroine* (female)

poet—not *poet* (male) and *poetess* (female)

sculptor—not *sculptor* (male) and *sculptress* (female)

Eliminating sexist pronoun use

The word *he* is not inclusive.

Like the all-encompassing use of *man* for all humanity, *he*, when used for all people, is quite literally wrong . . . and sometimes silly.

When an expert on women in the media was quoted in a major metropolitan daily about whether media women perceive different news stories from their male counterparts, an old, and sexist, pronoun preference was imposed, even though the speaker actually said "his or her":

"Each person sees life through his own experience," she adds. "Women in the newsroom—of newspapers and radio and television stations—do change the news."

There were no men in the story. The only appropriate singular pronoun would be *her. He* refers to men. *She* refers to women. *They* refers to both sexes. Using *he, him* and *his* for both sexes denies one sex.

The use of *he* has centuries of authority behind it, but it doesn't work today. The argument for using only *he* today is that *he and she* constructions are unwieldy. So what? It's more important to be factual than terse. But, it's usually easier to change to the plural *they.*

In fact, a case can be made for using *she* if only one pronoun is to be used: Because women are the majority of Americans, *she* more adequately conveys "everyone" than *he.* (Savvy, a magazine for executive women, does use *she* throughout as the generic pronoun, in direct opposition to the generic *he,* to convey information about all people.)

To test for sexism in the use of pronouns, use the feminine pronoun in place of the masculine to determine the appropriateness of the construction:

At the American Booksellers Convention, each of the 30 interviewed authors then signed her books for buyers.

Her does not include the male authors, just as *his* would not include female authors.

UNACCEPTABLE TERMS

Here are some terms *to avoid* (many of them are considered slurs) when writing or editing stories (and, of course, in *most instances* even when the preferable terms are suggested, they should not be used except when absolutely germane to the story).

Racial, ethnic, and religious

Bible thumper—offensive; meaning conservative Christian

brave—offensive term for male Native American

Chinaman/Chink—racial epithet for *Asian American* or *Chinese*

colored—unacceptable except as part of title: National Association for the Advancement of Colored People; *people of color*, however, is acceptable for non-Caucasians

cracker, hillbilly, Okie, redneck—offensive terms for those so described

dyke/butch/homo—offensive terms for *female homosexuals* or *lesbians*

faggot/queer/queen—offensive terms for *male homosexuals*

gook—offensive ethnic term for *Vietnamese* and all other Asian Americans

to gyp—offensive; term meaning to cheat, derived from gypsy

Hispanic—term denoting two dozen groups, not monolithic; use Mexican American, Cuban American, etc.

honky—offensive term directed toward whites by blacks

holy roller—offensive; use *fundamentalist*

Indian—an offensive term to many who call themselves *Native Americans* (despite The AP Stylebook's objection) or who tend to prefer even more their particular tribe's name (there are 443 tribes). Use American Indian in most cases. Also,

"Indians" is not used after a tribal name, e.g., "Navajo Indians" is redundant.

Indian—people of India, the Asian country; does not refer to people of the old British Indian Empire, such as Pakistanis, Sri Lankans, Burmese and Bangladeshis; do not use the term *East Indian*, a misnomer and colonialist term.

Indian-giver—offensive term for someone who gives something away, then takes it back

Jap—racial epithet for *Japanese*

JAP—derogatory term meaning Jewish American Princess

to Jew—an offensive term meaning to barter, implying an attempt to cheat someone, as presumably a Jew would do

kike—anti-Semitic term

Latin lover—offensive stereotype for those of Spanish background

mackerel snapper—offensive term for *Catholics*

Moonie—offensive; *member of the Unification Church*

Negro—use *black*

nigger—offensive term for *black*

Oreo—offensive term which indicates belief that another black is black outside but white inside; trademark for chocolate sandwich cookies with white filling

Oriental—derogatory; use *Asian American* or *Asian*

pickaninny/tar baby—offensive terms for *black children*

pollock—derogatory; use *Polish*

Red—offensive term for *Communists*

retard—offensive term for *retarded person*

spic—offensive ethnic term; use correct nationality

squaw—offensive term for female Native American

WASP—stereotype; White Anglo-Saxon Protestant

wetback—derogatory term for *Mexican Americans* or *Mexican*

wop/dago—derogatory for *Italians*

Do not use these words or the many similar terms for other groups.

Ageist

senior citizen—some, including John Simon, object to the term as "an unsavory euphemism," but it seems here to stay. Alternatives are *the aged, the old, the elderly, the retired.*

spry—clichéd description of the elderly that assumes most
   older people are decrepit
codger, gaffer—offensive in any context

The disabled

basket case—a term to avoid; offensive. The term began as British army slang for a quadruple amputee who had to be carried in a basket, but it has come to mean anyone who is
   incapacitated.
birth defect—instead use born with . . .
confined to a wheelchair—instead use person who uses a
   wheelchair
cripple/crippled by—offensive; disabled/physically disabled is
   preferable
deaf, mute—Do not use this or, worse, deaf and dumb. Many
   now prefer the term hearing-impaired or speech-impaired.
handicapped/handicap—instead use disabled/disability
inflicted—instead use caused by
normal—acceptable for statistics and average. Certainly not
   complimentary when referring to a disabled person as abnormal. Instead use non-disabled.
spastic—instead use person who has cerebral palsy
stricken with—instead use incurred a disability
restricted to a wheelchair—instead use person who uses a
   wheelchair
wheelchair bound—instead use person who uses a wheelchair

Important others

AIDS victim, AIDS sufferer—offensive; person living with AIDS
   or person with AIDS is preferable.
reformed alcoholic—offensive; both the American Medical Association and Alcoholics Anonymous treat alcoholism as an
   illness. Someone cannot reform from an illness; use recover-
   ing alcoholic.

What we have set out in this chapter is not easy to accomplish. Our
language is rife with judgmental, stereotypical and unfair terms.
Journalists play a key role in eliminating such terms from the
language. They should take every opportunity to do so.

Spelling

"It's a damn poor mind that can think of only one way to spell a word!"

—ANDREW JACKSON

That may have been true in Jackson's day, but in this age you are expected to be able to spell words correctly. This appendix is designed to help.

We begin with a few rules that, if remembered, will save you time by eliminating the need to look up many spellings. A list of frequently misspelled words follows. Learn as many of these as possible to reduce the time you spend with a dictionary. Finally, we have compiled rules of hyphenation and a useful reference list to help you determine whether something should be one word, two words or hyphenated.

RULES THAT SAVE TIME LOOKING UP WORDS

1. **Review the rules for plurals and possessives (Chapter 1, page 11).**
2. **Use *i* before *e* except after *c*. But there are some notable exceptions**:

   ancient, aweigh, beige, caffeine, counterfeit, financier, foreign, forfeit, heifer, height, inveigle, leisure, neighbor, neither, protein, science, seize, seizure, sleigh, sleight, sufficient, their, weigh, weight, weird.

3. Learn the effect of prefixes and suffixes on the spelling of words. A *prefix* is a syllable, group of syllables or word united with or joined to the beginning of a word to alter its meaning or to create a new word. For example, *il-* is a prefix added to *legal* to reverse its meaning to *illegal*. Prefixes usually have no effect on spelling of the root word.

A *suffix* is a sound, syllable or group of syllables added to the end of a word to change its meaning, give it grammatical function or form a new word. For example, *-ish* added to *small* creates *smallish; -ed* added to *walk* creates *walked*. Often suffixes do not change the spelling of a word, as these two examples suggest. In other cases, the spelling is affected.

Here are a few basic rules:

- Remember that *y* changes to *i* before the suffixes *-er* or *-est: happy, happier, happiest.*

- Change a final *y* to *i* before adding a suffix that begins with any vowel other than *i: likelihood, fiftyish.*

- Vowels (the letters *a, e, i, o, u* and sometimes *y*) and consonants (the other letters of the alphabet) also may affect spelling, depending on where they fall in the word. Usually, you double a final single consonant before adding a suffix that starts with a vowel if the root word is one syllable or the last syllable is stressed. If not, don't double the consonant.

  Examples of doubled consonants: *admitted, beginning, committed, deferred, dropped, forgettable, fulfilling, occurred, preferred, regrettable, transferred.* Examples of single consonants: *benefited, canceled, galloped, happening, traveled.* Exceptions to this rule are words with two vowels before the final consonant (*eaten, woolen*); words ending in *x* (*fixing, taxed*); and three other words: *handicapped, kidnapped, programmed.*

- Words ending in *-al* or *-ful* form adverbs by adding *-ly: carefully.* Words ending in *-ic* generally form adverbs by adding *-ally: basically.* Exception: *publicly.*

- A silent *e* on the end of a word usually is kept if the suffix starts with a consonant: *hopeful*; it is dropped if the suffix starts with a vowel: *hoping.* Exceptions: *European, dyeing.* If the silent *e* follows a *c* or a *g*, the *e* is usually dropped before a suffix that starts with a consonant (*acknowledgment, judgment*) but kept before a suffix that starts with a vowel (*advantageous, enforceable, knowledgeable, manageable, noticeable, outrageous*). Exception: *arrangement.*

- If a word has the prefix *dis-* or *mis-*, there should be two *s*'s only if the root starts with an *s: disappear, disappoint, disservice, misspell.*

- *Mimic, panic, picnic* and *traffic* add a *k* before the suffixes *-ed, -er* or *-ing.*

4. To decide whether a word should end in *-able* or *-ible,* remember that words that end in *-able* generally are ones that can stand alone without the suffix; words that end in *-ible* are generally ones that cannot stand alone without the suffix. Some *-able* words: *acceptable, adaptable, workable.* **If a word ends in a single *e*, drop the *e* before adding *-able:*** *likable,* *lovable, movable, salable.* **If a word ends in two *e's*, keep both when adding *able:*** *agreeable.*

Some *-ible* words: *credible, divisible, flexible, horrible, permissible, tangible, terrible.* **Add *-ible* if the root ends in a soft *c* sound, but first drop the final *e:*** *forcible.*

Exceptions to the above rules: *accessible, capable, collectible, durable, flexible, repressible, indispensable, responsible.*

5. To decide between *-ede* and *-eed,* remember that only five words take a double *e:* *deed, exceed, indeed, proceed, succeed.* Other words take *-ede: concede, intercede, precede, recede. Supersede* is the only word ending in *-sede.*

6. To decide whether a word should be spelled with a *c* or an *s*, remember that nouns usually have *c*, verbs *s*: *prophecy* (noun), *prophesy* (verb); *advice* (noun), *advise* (verb). Exceptions that are the same for both noun and verb: *license, practice.*

7. Don't subtract letters when words are joined together: *overrule, withhold.*

8. To decide between *-ary* and *-ery,* remember that only six common words end in *-ery:* *cemetery, confectionery, distillery, millinery, monastery* and *stationery* (paper). **Other than these, spell it *-ary*.**

9. To decide between *-efy* and *-ify,* remember that only four common words end in *-efy:* *liquefy, putrefy, rarefy* and *stupefy*. **Other than these, spell it *-ify*.**

Words Often Misspelled

A

a lot
aberration
abet
abhorrence
abridgment
abscess
acceptable
accessible
accessory
accidentally
accommodate
accumulate
achievement
acknowledge
acknowledgment
acoustics
acquaintance
acquit
acquitted
adherent
admissible
adviser
affidavit
aficionado
aggressor
all right
alleged
allotted
already
Alzheimer's disease
analysis
annihilate
anoint
antiquated
appalled
apparent

appearance
appellate
Arctic
argument
ascend
asinine
assassin
assistant
athlete
attendance
auxiliary

B

baccalaureate
bachelor
baker's dozen
bakers' yeast
ballistic
bankruptcy
barbiturate
barrenness
battalion
beggar
beginning
bellwether
benefited
benefiting
berserk
bona fide
broccoli

C

caffeine
calendar
caliber
campaign
canceled
cancellation
carburetor
caress
Caribbean

categorically
caterpillar
cemetery
centennial
chaise longue (not
    lounge)
changeable
chauffeur
chief
children's play
chitterlings
Cincinnati
circuit
citizens band
coconut
coed
collectible
colossal
commemorate
commitment
committal
committee
comparable
compatible
competent
conceit
conceive
confectioners' sugar
confident
congratulations
connoisseur
conquer
conscience
conscientious
conscious
consensus
consistent
controversy
convenient
coolly
corroborate
counterfeit

criticize
cruelly

D

deceit
deductible
defendant
defensible
definitely
deity
dependent
derring-do
descendant
descent
description
desiccate
desirable
desperately
deteriorate
deterrent
development
diaphragm
diarrhea
dietitian
difference
dilapidated
dilemma
dilettante
diphtheria
dirigible
disappear
disappoint
disastrous
discernible
discipline
disillusioned
dissension
disservice
dissociate
divisive
dos and don'ts

doughnut
drought
drowned
drunkenness
duly
dumbbell
dumbfounded
durable

E

ebb
ecstasy
eerie
eighth
elegant
eligible
embarrass
emphysema
employee
endeavor
environment
equipped
erroneous
especially
exaggerate
excitable
excusable
exhibition
exhilarating
existence
exorbitant
explanation
extraordinary
exuberant
eyeing

F

facetious
Fahrenheit
familiar

feasible
February
fierce
fiery
financier
firefighter
fluorescent
fluoride
forcible
forfeit
fortunately
forty
fourth
fraudulent
fuchsia
fulfill

G

gaiety
galloped
garish
garrulous
gaudy
gauge
genealogy
glamour
glamorous
goodbye
gorilla
grammar
grievance
guarantee
guard
guerrilla

H

handkerchief
harass
harebrained
harelip

height
heir
hemorrhage
hierarchy
hitchhiker
homicide
hygiene
hypocrisy
hysterical

I

ifs and buts
illegibly
illegitimate
immediately
impostor
inadmissible
inadvertent
inaugurate
inconvenience
incredible
independent
indispensable
inevitable
inflammation
inherent
innocence
innocuous
innuendo
inoculate
inseparable
insistence
insulation
intercede
interrupt
irascible
iridescent
irrelevant
irreligious
irresistible
irreverent

J

jeopardy
jewelry
judgment
judicious

K

keenness
khaki
kidnapped
kimono
knowledgeable

L

laboratory
laid
lambaste
legionnaire
legitimate
leisure
liability
liaison
license
lieutenant
lightning
likable
likelihood
liquefy
loathsome
loneliness
luscious

M

mah-jongg
maintenance
malarkey
manageable
maneuver
marijuana
marriage
marshal

mayonnaise
meander
medicine
medieval
Mediterranean
memento
menswear
merited
metallic
millionaire
mimicked
miniature
minuscule
miscellaneous
mischievous
missile
misspell
mollify
monastery
murmured
mystifying

N

naive
naphtha
necessary
neighbor
newsstand
nickel
niece
ninth
noticeable
nuisance

O

oblige
observer
occasion
occurred
occurrence
offense
offered

OK'd
omission
omitted
opportunity
oppressive
ordinarily
original
oscillate
overrule

P

paid
papier-mâché
paraffin
parallel
paralyzed
paraphernalia
parishioner
parliamentary
particularly
pastime
pavilion
peaceable
peculiarly
penicillin
percent
peremptory
permanent
permissible
perseverance
persistent
Philippines
physician
picnicking
pierce
pigeon
plaque
plausible
playwright
pneumonia
poinsettia
Portuguese

possession
practically
precede
predecessor
preferred
preparation
prerogative
presence
presumptuous
pretense
prevalence
preventive
primitive
privilege
procedure
proceed
prodigy
profited
propeller
prosecutor
prurient
publicly
purify
pursue

Q

quandary
quantity
quantum
quarreling
querulous
query
questionnaire
queue
quotient

R

rarefy
rarity
readable
receipt
receive

recommend
reconnaissance
reconnoiter
recur
referee
reference
referred
rehearsal
reign
relevant
religious
reminiscence
renovation
repetitious
repressible
reservoir
resistance
responsibility
restaurateur
resurrection
retinue
Reye's syndrome
rheumatism
rhyme
rhythm
ridiculous
rock 'n' roll

S

sacrilegious
salable
sanatorium
sanitarium
scissors
secession
seize
seizure
separate
sergeant
sheriff
short-lived
siege

sieve
signaled
silhouette
similar
sizable
skier
skiing
skillful
skulduggery
sleight-of-hand
soft-pedal
soldier
solicitor
soliloquy
soluble
soothe
sophomore
sovereign
spiraled
straitjacket
strictly
stupefy
subpoena
subtlety
subtly
succeed
successful
supersede
surfeit
surprise
surveillance
susceptible
symmetry
synonymous

T

tariff
teachers college
teen-age
teepee
temperamental
tendency

WORDS OFTEN MISSPELLED

tentacles
thoroughly
till
tinker's dam
tobacco
toboggan
tournament
tranquillity
transferral
transmitter
traveler
truly
Tucson
tumultuous
twelfth
tying
typing
tyrannous

U

ukulele
uncontrollable

undoubtedly
usable

V

vacancy
vacillate
vacuum
vengeance
verifiable
veterinary
vicious
victuals
vilify
villain
virtually
volume
voyageur
voyeur

W

Wednesday
weird

wherever
wholly
wield
wiener
willful
wiry
withhold
witticism
women's college
wondrous
woolen

X

X-ray

Z

zany
zucchini

WORDS OFTEN MISSPELLED

HYPHENATION AS A SPELLING PROBLEM

Rules for hyphenation

Writers and editors often are confused about whether a word is written as one word, as two words or with a hyphen. Here are some rules to remember that may help. The rules are followed by a useful reference list.

1. Suffixes are not hyphenated unless adding one would result in three l's in a row: *commencement, shell-less.*

Exception: Many compound adjectives, in which the "suffix" is really a separate word, are hyphenated: *penny-wise, street-wise.* Many compounds that use a preposition like *down, in, off, out, over* or *up* are also hyphenated: *break-in, carry-over, close-up, fade-out, send-off.*

Even so, many other compound words with prepositions at the end have dropped the hyphen: *breakup, fallout, holdover, takeoff.*

2. These prefixes are generally not hyphenated:

a (not, out)
ante (before)
anti (against)
bi (two)
by (near)—exception: *by-election*
dis (opposite)
full (complete)
hydro (water)
hyper (above, excessive)
infra (below)
inter (among, between)
intra (within)
mid (middle)
mini (small)
multi (many)
pan (all)

post (after)—exceptions: *post-bellum, post-mortem, post-obit*
pro (for)
re (again)—exceptions: When two different words would otherwise be spelled the same, hyphenate the one that means "again": *re-cover* (cover again), *re-creation* (a new creation)
semi
sub (under)
trans (across)
ultra (beyond)
un (not)
under (beneath)
up (above)

3. These prefixes generally are hyphenated:

after (following)—exception: no hyphen if used to form a noun
all (every)
co (with)—exceptions: AP says not to hyphenate when words do not "indicate occupation or status," but note that this description does not clarify its examples: *coed, coeducation, coequal, coexist, coexistence, cooperate, cooperative, coordinate, coordination*
ex (former)—exceptions: words that mean "out of," such as *excommunicate, expropriate*
like (similar)—exceptions: *likelihood, likeness, likewise*
non (not)—exceptions: *nonchalance, nonchalant, nondescript, nonentity, nonsense, nonsensical*
odd (unusual)—exception: *oddball*
off (away)—exceptions: *offbeat, offcast, offhand, offload, offprint, offset, offshoot, offshore, offside, offspring, offstage*
one (single)
pro (for)—exceptions: words that don't connote support for something, such as *produce, profile, pronoun*
self—exceptions: *selfish, selfless, selfsame*
well (very)
wide (completely)—exception: *widespread*

4. Words beginning with the prefixes *half* and *pre* are sometimes hyphenated, sometimes not. You'll just have to look them up. If they do not appear in Webster's New World, hyphenate them.
5. The prefix *vice* remains a separate word: *vice president*.
6. When a prefix is added to a number or a word that starts with a capital letter, use a hyphen after the prefix: *anti-American, mid-20s, pre-Colombian, trans-Atlantic*.

7. When a prefix is added to a word that starts with the same letter, use a hyphen after the prefix: *pre-election, pre-eminent, pre-empt, pre-establish, pre-exist, semi-invisible.*

Looking up words for hyphenation

To decide whether a word is one word, two words, or hyphenated, here's the procedure for looking it up:

1. Check The Associated Press Stylebook.
2. If it's not there, check Webster's New World Dictionary.
3. If it's not there, check Webster's Third New International Dictionary.
4. If it's not there, the word is two words as a noun or verb, hyphenated as an adjective.

Following these rules, we put together a list of commonly questioned words. This list is useful when deciding whether to hyphenate because it's quicker than running through that four-step procedure.

One Word, Two Words or Hyphenated?

A

able-bodied
about-face
aboveboard
absent-minded
ad-lib (n., v., adj.)
aftereffect
after-hours
afterthought
aide-de-camp
aides-de-camp
air base
air-conditioned
airline (but check individual name)
airmail
airport
air show

airtight
air time
airways
a la carte
a la king
a la mode
all ready (everyone is ready), already (by now)
all right
all time (n.), all-time (adj.)
alma mater
a lot
also-ran (n.)
anti-aircraft
anti-bias
antibiotic

antibody
anticlimax
antidote
antifreeze
antigen
antihistamine
anti-inflation
anti-intellectual
antiknock
anti-labor
antimatter
antimony
antiparticle
antipasto
antiperspirant
antiproton
antiseptic
antiserum
anti-slavery
anti-social
antithesis
antitoxin
antitrust
antitussive
anti-war
Aqua-Lung (trademark)
archbishop
arch-Democrat
archdiocese
archenemy
arch-Republican
archrival
art form
artifact
art work
ashcan
ashtray
attorney general
automaker
auto racing
autoworker
awe-struck

a while (noun as obj. of prep. or in
    phrases like ''a while ago'' or ''a
    while back''), awhile (adv.)

B

baby-sit
baby sitter
baby-sitting
backcountry
backhanded
back porch (n.), back-porch (adj.)
back seat (n.), backseat (adj.)
backstabbing
backstop
back street (n.), back-street (adj.)
backtrack
back up (v.), backup (n., adj.)
backwoods
back yard (v.), backyard (adj.)
bail out (v.), bailout (n.)
ball carrier
ballclub
ballpark
ballplayer
ball point pen
ballroom
Band-Aid (tradename)
bandleader
bank robber
barhop
barkeeper
barmaid
bar mitzvah
barrelhouse
barroom
barstool
basket case
bellybutton
best seller
best-selling
big-bang theory

ONE WORD, TWO WORDS
OR HYPHENATED?

big time (n.), big-time (adj.)
bird watching
bird's-eye
blackout
blast off (v.), blastoff (n., adj.)
blood bath
bloodhound
blow-dryer
blow up (v.), blowup (n.)
blue blood (n.)
blue-blooded (adj.)
blue chip stock
boardinghouse
boarding school
boardroom
bodybuilder
boldface
bona fide
bonbon
boo-boo
bookdealer
bookstore
boomtown
bowlegged
box office (n.), box-office (adj.)
boyfriend
brand-new
break dancing (n.), break-dancing
     (adj.)
breakdown
break in (v.), break-in (n., adj.)
breakthrough
break up (v.), breakup (n., adj.)
breast-feed
bricklayer
bridegroom
bridesmaid
brother-in-law
brothers-in-law
brownout
brussels sprouts
build up (v.), buildup (n., adj.)
bullet hole

bulletproof
bullfight
bullpen
bull's-eye
bundt cake
bushelbasket
businesslike
businessman
businesswoman
bus line
busload
buy out (n., v.)
by-election
bylaw
byline
bypass
byproduct
bystreet

C

cabdriver
cabinetmaker
cakewalk
call up (v.), call-up (n., adj.)
candleholder
candlemaker
candymaker
cannot
card maker
carefree
caretaker
carmaker
car pool
carport
carry over (v.), carry-over (n., adj.)
car seat
carsick
carwash
caseload
cashbox
cash flow
cast member

catch all (v.), catchall (n., adj.)

cease fire (v.), cease-fire (n., adj.)

centerfold

cha-cha

chain saw

chairman

chairwoman

change over (v.), changeover (n.)

change up (v.), change-up (n., adj.)

check up (v.), checkup (n.)

cheese maker

chock-full

chowhound

Christmastime

churchgoer

church member

citizens band

city hall

citywide

claptrap

clean-cut

clean up (v.), cleanup (n., adj.)

clear-cut

clearinghouse

cloak-and-dagger

closed shop

close-up (n., adj.)

coal mine, coal miners

coastline

coatdress

coattails

co-author

Coca-Cola (trademark)

co-chairman

coconut

coed

coeducation

coequal

coexist

coexistence

coffee grinder

coffee maker

coffeepot

coffee table (n.), coffee-table (adj.)

co-host

coleslaw

collectors' item

colorblind

commander in chief

concertgoer

congressman

congresswoman

con man

cooperate

coordinate

coordination

co-owner

co-partner

co-pilot

cop-out

copy desk

copy editor

co-respondent

cornstarch

co-signer

co-star

cost-effective

countdown

counteract

countercharge

counterfoil

counterintelligence

counterproposal

counterspy

counter top (n.), counter-top (adj.)

countryside

country-western music

court-martial

courtroom

cover up (v.), cover-up (n., adj.)

co-worker

crack up (v.), crackup (n., adj.)

crawfish

crawl space

crew member

crisscross

crock pot
cropland
cross country (n.), cross-country
    (adj.)
cross-examination
cross-examine
cross-eye
cross fire
cross over (v.), crossover (n., adj.)
cross section (n.), cross-section (v.)
curtain raiser
custom-made
cut back (v.), cutback (n., adj.)
cut off (v.), cutoff (n., adj.)
cutoffs
cut out (v.), cutout (n.)

D

dark horse
date line (the international one),
    dateline (on a news story)
daylong
daytime
day to day (adv.), day-to-day (adj.)
D-day
dead center
dead end (n.), dead-end (adj.)
deathbed
decade-long
decision maker
decision-making (adj.)
Deepfreeze (trademark)
deep-sea (adj.)
deep water (n.), deep-water (adj.)
degree-day
derring-do
desk top (n.), desk-top (adj.)
die-hard (n., adj.)
dinner table
ditchdigger
docudrama
doghouse

dollhouse
door to door (n.), door-to-door (adj.)
double bind
double-check
double-faced
double-parked (n., v., adj.)
downdraft
down-home
downside
drive in (v.), drive-in (n., adj.)
drop out (v.), dropout (n.)
dump truck
Dutch oven
Dutch treat
dyed-in-the-wool (adj.)

E

earmark (v.)
easygoing
editor in chief
empty-handed
en route
even-steven
every day (adv.), everyday (adj.)
every one (each individual item),
    everyone (all people)
extra-base hit
extra-dry
extra-large
extralegal
extramarital
extra-mild
extraterrestrial
extraterritorial
eyesore
eye to eye (adv.), eye-to-eye (adj.)
eyewitness

F

face lift
face to face (adv.), face-to-face (adj.)
fact-finding

fade out (v.), fade-out (n.)

fall out (v.), fallout (n.)

far-fetched

far-flung

farmhouse

farmland

farm worker

far-off

far-ranging

farsighted

father-in-law

feather bedding (mattress), feather-bedding (union practice)

Ferris wheel

ferryboat

Fiberglas (trademark), fiberglass (generic)

field house

field trip

fieldwork

filmgoer

filmmaker

filmmaking (n.), film-making (adj.)

film ratings

fingertip

fire breather

fire chief

firefighter

fireproof

firetruck

fire wagon

firsthand

fistfight

flagpole

flagship

flameout

flare up (v.), flare-up (v.)

flea market

flimflam

flip-flop

floor-length

flower girl

flyswatter

folk singer

folk song

follow-through

follow up (v.), follow-up (n., adj.)

foolproof

foot-and-mouth disease

forebrain

forecast

foregoing

foretooth

fore-topgallant

fore-topmast

fore-topsail

fortuneteller

fortunetelling

forty-niner or '49er

foul-up (n.), foul up (v.)

four-flush

Four-H Club or 4-H Club

4-H'er

fraidycat

frame up (v.), frame-up (n.)

free-for-all

free-lance (v., adj.)

free-lancer (n.)

free on board

freestanding

freewheeling

freewill offering

freeze-dried

freeze-dry

freeze-drying

front line (n.), front-line (adj.)

front page (n.), front-page (adj.)

front-runner

fruit grower

full-dress

full-fledged

full house

full-length

full page (n.), full-page (adj.)

full-scale

full-size (adj.)

full time (n.), full-time (adj.)
fund-raiser (n.)
fund raising (n.), fund-raising (adj.)

G

game plan
get together (v.), get-together (n.)
gift wrap (n.), gift-wrap (v.)
giveaway
go ahead (v.), go-ahead (n.)
godchild
goddaughter
go-go
goodbye
goose bumps
granddad
granddaughter
grant-in-aid
grants-in-aid
groundbreaking
ground rules
groundskeeper
groundswell
ground water
grown-up (n., adj.)
G-string
guesthouse
gunbattle
gunboat
gunfight
gunfire
gunpoint
gunpowder

H

hair dryer
hairsbreadth
hairstyle
hairstyling
hairstylist
halfback

half-baked
half-blood
half brother
half-cocked
half dollar
halfhearted
half-hour (n., adj.)
half-life
half-mast
half-moon
half note
half sister
half size (n.), half-size (adj.)
half sole (n.), half-sole (v.)
half-staff
half tide
halftime
halftone
halftrack
half-truth
hand-carved
handcrafted
hand-held
handhold
handmade
hand-painted
hand-picked
hand-set (v.), handset (n.)
hand-sewn
hands off (n.), hands-off (adj.)
hand-stitched
hand to hand (n.), hand-to-hand (adj.)
hand to mouth (n.), hand-to-mouth
    (adj.)
hand warmers
handwrought
hangover
hang up (v.), hang-up (n.)
hanky-panky
hardback
hard-bound
hard-cover

hard-line
hardworking
harebrained
harelip
has been (v.), has-been (n.)
H-bomb
headache
headlong
head-on
heartbeat
heartfelt
heart-rending
heartwarming
helter-skelter
heyday
hideaway
hide out (v.), hide-out (n.)
hi-fi
higher-up
high jinks
high point
high-rise (n., adj.)
high-step (v.)
high-stepper
hit and run (v.), hit-and-run (n., adj.)
hitchhike
hitchhiker
hit man
hocus-pocus
hodgepodge
ho-hum
hold over (v.), holdover (n.)
hold up (v.), holdup (n., adj.)
home-baked
home builder
home buyer
home-grown
homemade
homemaker
homeowner
hometown
hook up (v.), hookup (n.)

horsepower
horse race
horse rider
horse-trader
hotbed
hotheaded
hot line
hot seat
hot spot
hot tub
hour-long
house call
housecleaning
household
househusband
houseplant
hurly-burly
hush-hush
hydroelectric
hyperactive
hypercritical

I

ice storm
inasmuch
inbound
in-depth
Indochina
indoor (adj.), indoors (adv.)
infield
infighting
infrared
infrastructure
in-group
in-house
in-law
inpatient (n., adj.)
insofar
inter-American
interracial
interstate

intramural
intrastate

J

jai alai
jerry-built
jetliner
jet plane
job hunting (n.), job-hunting (adj,)
jukebox
jumbo jet
jury-rigged

K

K mart
kick off (v.), kickoff (n.)
kilowatt-hour
kindhearted
knock off (v.), knock-off (n.)
know-how
kowtow

L

lamebrain
lame duck (n.), lame-duck (adj.)
last-ditch effort
latecomer
lawsuit
left-handed
left-hander
left wing (n.), left-wing (adj.)
let up (v.), letup (n., adj.)
life jacket
lifelike
lifelong
Life Savers (trademark), lifesaver
life-size
lifestyle
lifetime
life vest
lift off (v.), liftoff (n.)

light bulb
lighthearted
light-year
like-minded
like-natured
likewise
long distance (n.), long-distance
    (adj., or in reference to phone
    calls)
long-lasting
long-lived
long-range
long-run
long shot (n.), long-shot (adj.)
longstanding
long term (n.), long-term (adj.)
long time (n.), longtime (adj.)
look-alike
lovemaking
lumberyard
lunch box
lunchtime

M

machine gun (n.), machine-gun
    (adj., v.)
machine-gunner
machine-made
mah-jongg
makeshift
make up (v.), makeup (n., adj.)
man-made
map maker
meatball
meatcutter
meat loaf
menage a trois
menswear
merry-go-round
metalwork
mid-America
mid-Atlantic

midsemester
midterm
mind-set
mine shaft
minibus
miniseries
miniskirt
mix up (v.), mix-up (n., adj.)
mock-up (n.)
moneymaker
money-saving
monthlong
mop up (v.), mop-up (n., adj.)
mother-in-law
motor home
mountain man
mousehole
moviegoer
movie house
moviemaker
moviemaking
mud slide
multicolored
multilateral
multimillion
multimillionaire
muscle ache
mythmaking

N

nail clippers
name tag
narrow gauge (n.), narrow-gauge (adj.)
narrow-minded
nationwide
nerve-racking
newfangled
newsmagazine
newsroom
newsstand
news writer

news writing
new wave (n.), new-wave (adj.)
nickname
nightclub
night shift
nightspot
nighttime
nitpicking
nitty-gritty
non-aligned
nonchalance
nonchalant
nondescript
nonentity
non-restrictive
nonsense
nonsensical
no one

O

oceangoing
oddsmaker
off-Broadway
off-color
off-duty
offhand
off-off-Broadway
off-peak
off-road
off-season
offset
offshore
offside
offstage
off-white
oilman
old-time
old-timer
old times
Old West
Old World
one-sided

one time (n.), one-time (adj.)
ongoing
on-line
open-minded
outact
outargue
outbluff
outbox
outbrag
outclimb
outdated
outdistance
outdrink
outeat
outfield
outfight
outfox
outhit
outleap
outmatch
out of bounds (n.), out-of-bounds
   (adj.)
out of court (adv.), out-of-court (adj.)
outpatient (n., adj.)
outperform
outpitch
outpost
outproduce
output
outquote
outrace
outscore
outshout
outstrip
outswim
outtalk
outwalk
oven-proof
overall
overbuy
overexert
overrate
override

oversize
overtime
overview

P

pacemaker
pacesetter
paddy wagon
painkiller
panchromatic
pantheism
pantsuit
pantyhose
paper bag
paper clip
paper towel
paperwork
Pap test (or smear)
pari-mutuel
parkland
part time (adv.), part-time (adj.)
partygoer
passer-by
patrolman
patrolwoman
paycheck
payday
payload
peacekeeper
peacekeeping
peacemaker
peacemaking
peace offering
peacetime
pell-mell
penny-wise
pen pal
percent
pet store
petty officer
pile up (v.), pileup (n., adj.)
pillowcase

pinch hit

pingpong (table tennis), Ping-Pong (trademark)

pin up (v.), pinup (n.)

pipeline

place mat

playoff

pocketbook

pocket watch

point-blank

police officer

policyholder

policy-maker

policy-making (n., adj.)

pom-pom (weapon), pompon (cheerleader paraphernalia)

pooh-pooh

postcard

postdate

postdoctoral

postelection

postgraduate

postnuptial

post office

postoperative

postscript

postwar

pothole

potluck

potshot

powder keg

power line

prearrange

precondition

pre-convention

precook

pre-cut

predate

pre-dawn

predispose

pre-election

pre-eminent

pre-empt

pre-establish

pre-exist

prefix

preflight

preheat

prehistoric

preignition

prejudge

premarital

pre-menstrual

prenatal

pre-register

preschool

preset

pretest

pretrial

prewar

pre-wash

price tag

prima-facie (adj.)

prizewinner

prizewinning

pro-business

profit-sharing (n., adj.)

pro-labor

pro-life

pro-war

pull back (v.), pullback (n.)

pull out (v.), pullout (n.)

purebred

push-button (n., adj.)

push up (v.), push-up (n., adj.)

put out (v.), putout (n.)

Q

Q-and-A format

QE2

quick-witted

R

rainstorm

ranch house

ONE WORD, TWO WORDS OR HYPHENATED?

211

ranchland
rangeland
rank and file (n.), rank-and-file (adj.)
rawhide
razor strop
razzle-dazzle
razzmatazz
ready-made
rearview mirror
recover (regain), re-cover (cover
    again)
red-haired
red-handed (adj., adv.)
red-hot
redneck
re-elect
re-election
re-emerge
re-employ
re-enact
re-engage
re-enlist
re-enter
re-entry
re-equip
re-establish
re-examine
reform (improve), re-form (form
    again)
rendezvous
resign (quit), re-sign (sign again)
riffraff
right hand (n.)
right-handed (adj.)
right-hander (n.)
right-to-work
right wing (n.), right-wing (adj.)
ring bearer
rip off (v.), rip-off (n., adj.)
riverboat
roadside
rock 'n' roll
roll call (n.), roll-call (adj.)

roller coaster
roller skate (n.), roller-skate (v.)
roly-poly
round table (n.), round-table (adj.)
round trip (n.), round-trip (adj.)
round up (v.), round-up (n.)
rubber band
rundown
runner-up
running mate
rush hour (n.), rush-hour (adj.)

S

safe-deposit box (not safety-deposit
    box)
sales pitch
sandbag
sandstorm
saucepan
school bus
schoolteacher
scot-free
seat belt (n.), seat-belt (adj.)
seawater
second guess (n.), second-quess (v.)
second-guesser
second hand (n.), secondhand (adj.,
    adv.)
second-rate
secretary-treasurer
seesaw
self-assured
self-defense
self-esteem
semiannual
semicolon
send off (v.), send-off (n.)
set up (v.), setup (n., adj.)
7-Eleven (trademark)
Seven-Up or 7UP (trademarks)
sewer line
shake up (v.), shake-up (n., adj.)

shape up (v.), shape-up (n., adj.)
Sheetrock (trademark)
shirt sleeve (n.), shirt-sleeve (adj.)
shoeshine
shoestring
shootout (v.), shoot-out (n.)
shopworn
shortchange
short-handed
short-lived
shotgun
showcase
show off (v.), showoff (n.)
showroom
showstopper
shut down (v.), shutdown (n.)
shut in (v.), shut-in (n.)
shut off (v.), shut-off (n.)
side by side (adv.), side-by-side (adj.)
side dish
side effect
sidestep
side street (n.)
sidetrack
side trip
sightseeing
sightseer
sign up (v. or n.)
single-handed
single-handedly
sister-in-law
sisters-in-law
sit down (v.), sit-down (n., adj.)
sit in (v.), sit-in (n., adj.)
skyrocketing
slantwise
sledgehammer
sleight of hand (n.), sleight-of-hand (adj.)
slide show
slowdown
slumlord
slush fund

small-arms fire
smash up (v.), smashup (n., adj.)
smoke bomb
smoke screen
snowdrift
snowfall
snowflake
snowman
snowplow
snowshoe
snowstorm
snowsuit
so called (adv.), so-called (adj.)
soft-cover
soft-pedal (not soft-peddle)
soft-spoken
songwriter
son-in-law
sound stage
sound track (n.), sound-track (adj.)
spacecraft
spaceship
space shuttle
speechmaker
speechmaking
speech writer
speech writing
speed up (v.), speedup (n., adj.)
sportswear
spot-check
spotlight
stained glass (n.), stained-glass (adj.)
standard-bearer
stand in (v.), stand-in (n., adj.)
standing room only
stand off (v.), standoff (n., adj.)
stand out (v.), standout (n., adj.)
stand up (v.), stand-up (adj.)
start up (v.), start-up (n., adj.)
statehouse
state police
states' rights
statewide

ONE WORD, TWO WORDS
OR HYPHENATED?

station wagon
stepbrother
stepchild
stepdaughter
step family
stepfather
stepmother
stepparent
steppingstone
stepsister
stepson
stockbroker
stone carver
stool pigeon
stopgap
stop off (v.), stop-off (n)
stopover
story line
storyteller
stove top (n.), stove-top (adj.)
straight-laced (strict, severe)
strait-laced (pertaining to confine-
    ment, as a corset)
straitjacket
street dance
street gang
streetlamp
streetlight
street people
street-smart
street sweeper
streetwalker
street wise
strikebreaker
strong-arm (v., adj.)
strong-willed
subbasement
subcommittee
subculture
subdivision
submachine gun
suborbital
subtotal

subzero
summertime
sundress
sun porch
superagency
supercarrier
supercharge
superhighway
superpower
supersonic
supertanker
supragovernmental
supranational
sweat pants
sweat shirt
sweat suit

T

tablecloth
tablespoon
table tennis
taillight
tailspin
tail wind
take-home pay
take off (v.), takeoff (n., adj.)
take out (v.), takeout (n., adj.)
take over (v.), takeover (n., adj.)
take up (v.), takeup (n., adj.)
tape-record (v.), tape recording (n.)
task force
tattletale
teachers college
teakettle
teammate
tear gas
teaspoon
teen-age (adj.; note: no *d* on end)
teen-ager
TelePrompTer (trademark)
telex (generic), Telex (name)
telltale

tenderhearted
tenfold
terry cloth
theatergoer
Third World
3-D
three R's
throw away (v.), throwaway (n., adj.)
thumbtack
thunderstorm
tidbit
tiebreaker
tie in (v.), tie-in (n., adj.)
tie up (v.), tie-up (n., adj.)
timesaver
timesaving
time sharing (n.), time-sharing (adj.)
timetable
tiptop
titleholder
tollhouse
Tommy gun (trademark)
top-notch
touch up (v.), touch-up (n., adj.)
toy makers
trade in (v.), trade-in (n., adj.)
trademark
trade off (v.), trade-off (n., adj.)
transcontinental
transmigrate
transoceanic
transsexual
transship
trans-Atlantic
trans-Pacific
trash can
trendsetter
trigger-happy
truck driver
truck stop
try out (v.), tryout (n.)
T-shirt
tune up (v.), tuneup (n., adj.)

turboprop
turn off (v.), turnoff (n.)
turnpike
twofold

U

U-boat
ultrahigh frequency
ultra-leftist
ultramodern
ultranationalism
ultra-rightist
ultrasonic
ultraviolet
un-American
unarmed
undersheriff
undersold
under way (all senses but nautical), underway (in nautical sense when used as an adjective before a word, as in "underway flotilla")
upper hand
upside down (adv.), upside-down (adj.)
upstate
up-tempo
upward
U-turn

V

V-8
vice chancellor
vice consul
vice president
vice principal
vice regent
vice secretary
vice versa
videocassette (n., adj.)

ONE WORD, TWO WORDS OR HYPHENATED?

videodisc
video game
videotape (n., v.)
V-J Day
V-neck
voodoo
vote-getter

W

wagonmaker
wagon master
walk on (v.), walk-on (n.)
walk up (v.), walk-up (n., adj.)
wall covering
wall hanging
warhead
war horse (horse), warhorse (veteran)
warlike
warlord
warmhearted
warm-up
wartime
washed up (v.), washed-up (adj.)
wash out (v.), washout (n.)
wastebasket
wastepaper
waste water
water bed
watercolor
waterline
watershed
water ski (n.), water-ski (v.)
water-skier
water-skiing
waterspout
water tank
weak-kneed
weather-beaten
weatherman
weather vane
weekend

weeklong
week-nights
weightlifting
well-being
well-to-do
well-wishers
wet bar
wheelchair
wheeler-dealer
whereabouts
wherever
whirlwind
white collar (n.), white-collar (adj.)
white paper
whitewash (n., v., adj.)
white water (n.), white-water (adj.)
wholehearted
wholesale price index
whole-wheat
wide-angle
wide-awake
wide-brimmed
wide-eyed
wide-open
widespread
wife beater
willpower
wind chill index
wind power
window-dress (v.)
window dressing (n.)
window-shop (v.)
window-shopping
wind-swept
wind up (v.), windup (n., adj.)
winemaker
winemaking
wine taster
wingspan
winter storm warning
winter storm watch
wintertime
wiretap

wood-burning (as in wood-burning
    stove, woodburning (as in wood-
    burning kit)
woodcarver
woodcarving
wood heat
woodsmoke
woodstove (our rule)
woodwork
word-of-mouth (n., adj.)
workday
work force
working class (n.), working-class
    (adj.)
workout
workplace
workweek
worldwide
worn-out

write in (v.), write-in (n., adj.)
wrongdoing

X

X-ray

Y

yard sale
year-end (adj.)
yearlong
year-round
yesteryear
yo-yo
yuletide

Z

zigzag

Wire-Service Style Summary

Most publications adhere to rules of style to avoid annoying inconsistencies. Without a stylebook to provide guidance in such matters, writers would not know whether the word *president* should be capitalized when preceding or following a name; whether the correct spelling is *employee* or *employe* (dictionaries list both); or whether a street name should be *Twelfth* or *12th*.

Newspapers use the wire-service stylebooks to provide such guidance. For consistency, The Associated Press and United Press International collaborated in establishing style, and the rules of the two services differ only in minor ways. Most newspapers follow one of those stylebooks, although Associated Press dominates. This appendix is an abbreviated summary of the primary rules of wire-service style. (For more punctuation rules, see Chapter 6.)

About 10 percent of the rules in the stylebook account for 90 percent of the wire-service style you will use regularly. The rest of the rules will be used about 10 percent of the time. It makes sense, then, to first learn those rules that you will use most often. This appendix includes the rules used most frequently, arranged by topic to make them easier to learn.

Wire-Service Style Summary

ABBREVIATIONS AND ACRONYMS

1. Punctuation of abbreviations

- Generally speaking, abbreviations of two letters or fewer use periods: *600 B.C., A.D. 1066, 8 a.m., 7 p.m., U.N., U.S., R.I., N.Y., 8151 Yosemite St.* Exceptions: *AM radio, FM radio, 35mm camera, The AP Stylebook, "LA smog," D-Mass., R-Kan., IQ, TV.*

- Generally speaking, abbreviations of three letters or more do not use periods: *CIA, FBI, NATO, mpg, mph.* Exceptions: *c.o.d., U.S.S.R.*

2. Symbols

%—Always write out as *percent* in a story, but you may use the symbol in a headline

&—Always write out as *and* unless it is an actual part of a company's formal name.

¢—Always write out as *cent* or *cents*.

$—Always use the symbol rather than the word with any actual figure, and put the symbol before the figure. Write out *dollar* only if you are speaking of, say, the value of the dollar on the world market.

3. Dates

- Never abbreviate days of the week.
- Don't abbreviate a month unless it has a date of the month with it: *August; August 1987; Aug. 25; Aug. 25, 1987.*
- The five months spelled with five letters or fewer are never abbreviated: *March; April 20; May 13, 1987; June 1956; July of that year.*
- Never abbreviate *Christmas* as *Xmas*, even in a headline.
- *Fourth of July* is written out.

4. People and titles

- Courtesy titles (*Mr., Miss, Mrs., Ms.*) are not used except on second reference in stories mentioning husband and wife. They should also be retained in a quotation when someone else uses them. Some newspapers make exceptions, using them, for example, in obituaries.
- The abbreviations *Gov., Lt. Gov., Rep., Sen., the Rev.* and military titles are used on first reference, then the title is dropped on subsequent references. Some titles you might expect to see abbreviated before a name are not abbreviated in AP style: *Attorney General, District Attorney, President, Professor and Superintendent.*
- The abbreviations *Jr.* and *Sr.* are used behind a name on first reference if appropriate, but they are not set off by commas as you learned to do in English class.

5. Organizations

- The first reference for most organizations is written out in full rather than using an acronym: *National Organization of Women.* For *CIA, FBI and GOP*, however, the acronym may be used on first reference.

- Well-known abbreviations such as FCC and NOW may be used in headlines even though they would not be acceptable on first reference in the story.

- Do not put the abbreviation of an organization in parentheses behind the full name on first reference. If its abbreviation is that confusing, don't use an abbreviation at all but rather call it something like "the gay rights group" or "the bureau" on second reference.

- The abbreviations *Co., Cos., Corp., Inc.* and *Ltd.* are used at the end of a company's name even if the company spells the word out; they are not abbreviated if followed by other words such as "of America." The abbreviations *Co., Cos.* and *Corp.* are still abbreviated, however, if followed by *Inc.* or *Ltd.* (and, by the way, these latter two abbreviations are not set off by commas even if the company uses commas).

- Political affiliations are abbreviated after a name in the following way: "Sen. John Danforth, R-Mo., said . . ." Note the use of a single letter without a period for the party and the use of commas around the party and state.

- The word *association* is never abbreviated, even as part of a name.

6. Places

- Don't abbreviate a state name unless it follows the name of a city in that state: *Nevada; Brown City, Mich.*

- The six states spelled with five letters or fewer are never abbreviated, nor are the two non-contiguous states: *Alaska, Hawaii, Idaho, Iowa, Maine, Ohio, Texas, Utah.*

- State abbreviations used are the old-fashioned ones—not the post office's two-letter ones: *Miss.*, not *MS.*

The proper state abbreviations are:

Ala.	Kan.	Nev.	R.I.
Ariz.	Ky.	N.H.	S.C.
Ark.	La.	N.J.	S.D.
Calif.	Md.	N.M.	Tenn.
Colo.	Mass.	N.Y.	Vt.
Conn.	Mich.	N.C.	Va.
Del.	Minn.	N.D.	Wash.
Fla.	Miss.	Okla.	W.Va.
Ga.	Mo.	Ore.	Wis.
Ill.	Mont.	Pa.	Wyo.
Ind.	Neb.		

- Domestic towns and cities are followed by their state's abbreviation unless they appear in the AP list of cities that stand alone. Many publications add to AP's list their own list of towns well-known in their state or region. Foreign towns and cities are followed by their nation's full name unless they appear in the AP dateline list of cities that stand alone. Once a state or nation has been identified in the story, it is unnecessary to repeat it unless clarity demands it.

- The names of thoroughfares are not abbreviated if there is no street address with them: *Main Street, Century Boulevard West.*

- If the thoroughfare's name has the words *avenue, boulevard, street,* or any of the directions on a map, such as *north* or *southeast,* those words are abbreviated with a street address: *1044 W. Maple St., 1424 Lee Blvd. S., 999 Jackson Ave.*

- In a highway's name, *U.S.* is always abbreviated, but a state's name never is. In the case of an interstate highway, the name is written in full on first reference, abbreviated on subsequent ones: *Interstate 70* (first reference), *I-70* (second reference).

- *Fort* and *Mount* are never abbreviated. The abbreviation *St.* for Saint is always used in place names, however, with the exception of Saint John in New Brunswick, Ste. Genevieve in Missouri and Sault Ste. Marie in Michigan and Ontario.

- Abbreviate United States and United Nations as *U.S.* and *U.N.* when used as adjectives, but spell them out as nouns.

7. Miscellaneous

- *IQ*: No periods; acceptable in all references to intelligence quotient.

- *No. 1, No. 2*, etc.: Abbreviate and capitalize the word *number* when followed by a numeral.

- *TV*: No periods. Do not use except in headlines and in constructions such as "cable TV."

- *UFO*: Acceptable in all references to an unidentified flying object.

- *vs.*: Don't abbreviate *versus* as *v.*

CAPITALIZATION

1. General rule: Proper nouns are capitalized; common nouns are not. Unfortunately, this is not always so easy as it sounds.

- With animals, food and plants, capitalize only the parts of a compound name that would be capitalized by themselves:

German shepherd, basset hound; Boston cream pie, chocolate fudge supreme; Dutch elm, lily of the valley.

Exceptions: brussels sprouts, french fries, graham crackers, manhattan cocktail.

- Beware of trade names that are often mistakenly used generically. (See also Chapter 1, pages **16–17**.)

2. Regions are capitalized, but directions are not: *We drove east two miles to catch the interstate out West*.

- Adjectives and nouns pertaining to a region are capitalized: *Southern accent, Western movie, a Southerner, a Western*.
- A region combined with a country's name is not capitalized unless that is the name of a divided country: *eastern United States, West Germany*.
- A region combined with a state name is capitalized only if it is famous: *Southern California, southern Colorado*.

3. When two or more compound proper nouns are combined to share a word in common made plural, the shared plural is lowercase:

Missouri and Mississippi rivers; Chrisman and Truman high schools.

4. Government and college terms are not always as consistent as you might think.

- Departments. College departments follow the animal, food and plant rule, capitalizing only words already proper nouns in themselves: *Spanish department, sociology department*. But a specific government department is always capitalized, even without the city, state or federal designator, and even if turned around with *of* deleted:

  Police Department, Fire Department, State Department.

- Committees. College and government committees are capitalized if the formal name is given rather than a shorter, descriptive designation: *Special Senate Select Committee to Investigate Improper Labor-Management Practices, rackets committee*.

- Degrees. Academic degrees are spelled out and lowercase: *bachelor of arts degree, master's degree*. Avoid the abbreviations *Ph.D., M.A., B.A.,* etc., except in lists.

- Always capitalized (unless plural or generic): *City Council, County Commission* (but alone, *council* and *commission* are lowercase). *Cabinet* is always capitalized when referring to advisers. *Legislature* is capitalized if the state's body is formally named that. *Capitol*, the building, is always capitalized, but *capital*, the city, is not.

- Never capitalized: *board of directors, board of trustees* (but *Board of Curators* and *Board of Education* are capitalized). *Federal, government* and *administration* are not capitalized. *President* and *vice president* are capitalized only before a name.

- Military titles (*Sgt. Maj., Gen.*) before a name are capitalized, as are *Air Force, Army, Marines* and *Navy* if referring to U.S. forces.

- Political parties are capitalized, including the word *party: Democratic Party, Socialist Party*. Be sure, however, to capitalize words like *communist, democratic, fascist* and *socialist* only if they refer to a formal party rather than a philosophy.

5. Religion. Lowercase *pope* unless before a name, but *Mass* is always uppercase. Pronouns for God or Jesus are lowercase. *Bible* is capitalized if meaning the Holy Scriptures, and lowercased when referring to another book: *a hunter's bible*. Sacraments are capitalized if they commemorate events in the life of Jesus or signify his presence: *baptism, Communion*.

6. Races. Actual race names are capitalized, but color descriptions are not:

Caucasian, Mongoloid, Negro; white, red, black.

7. Formal titles of people are capitalized before a name, but occupational titles are not:

President Reagan, Mayor Andrew Young, Coach Bear Bryant, astronaut Ed White. Some are not easy to tell apart: managing editor, chief executive officer; when in doubt, put the title behind the name, set off with commas, and use lowercase.

8. The first word in a direct quotation is capitalized only if the quote meets all these criteria:

- It is a complete sentence. Don't capitalize a partial quote.

- It stands alone as a separate sentence or paragraph, or is set off from its source by a comma or colon.

- It is a direct quotation (in quotation marks).

9. A question within a sentence is capitalized:

My only question is, When do we start?

NUMERALS

1. Cardinal numbers (numerals) are used in:

- Addresses. Always use numerals for street addresses: *1322 N. 10th St.*
- Ages. Always use numerals, even for days or months: *3 days old; John Burnside, 56.*
- Aircraft and spacecraft: *F-4, DC-10, Apollo 11*; exception: *Air Force One.*
- Clothes size: size 6
- Dates. Always use the numeral alone—no *-rd, -st* or *-th* behind it.
- Dimensions: *5-foot 6-inch guard* (but no hyphen when the word modified is one associated with size, such as *3 feet tall, 10 feet long*).
- Highways: *U.S. 63*
- Millions, billions and trillions use a numeral before the word: *1.2 billion.*
- Money. Always use numerals, but starting with a million, write like this: *$1.4 million.*
- Number: *No. 1, No. 2*
- Percentages. Always use numerals except at the beginning of a sentence.
- Recipes. Even amounts of less than 10 take numerals.
- Speeds: *55 mph, 4 knots*
- Sports. Use numerals for just about everything: *score 8-6, 2 yards, 3-under-par, 2 strokes.*
- Temperatures. All are numerals but *zero*; below zero, spell out *minus: minus 6*, not − 6 (except in tabular data).
- Time: *4 a.m., 6:32 p.m.*; but *noon, midnight, five minutes, three hours.*
- Weights: *7 pounds, 11 ounces*
- Years. Use numerals without commas: A date is the only numeral that can start a sentence: *1988 was a good year.; decade of the '80s*

2. Numerals with the suffixes *-nd, -rd, -st* and *-th* are used for:

- Political divisions (precincts, wards, districts): *3rd Congressional District*
- Military sequences: *1st Lt., 2nd Division, 7th Fleet*

- Courts: *2nd District Court; 10th Circuit Court of Appeals*
- Streets after Ninth. For First through Ninth, use words: Fifth Avenue, 13th Street.
- Amendments to the Constitution after *Ninth*. For First through Ninth, use words.

3. Words are used instead of numerals for:

- Numbers of less than 10, not excepted above
- Any number at the start of a sentence except for a year
- Casual numbers: *about a hundred or so*
- Fractions less than one: *one-half*

4. Use mixed numbers for fractions greater than one:

1 1/2

5. Use Roman numerals for a man who is the third or later in his family to bear a name, and for a king, queen, pope or world war:

John D. Rockefeller III, Pope John Paul II, Queen Elizabeth II, World War I

Bibliography

Abbott, Jeanne. *Basic Sentence Elements*. Columbia, Mo.: n.p., 1988.

Adorni, Sergio, and Primorac, Karen. *English Grammar for Students of Italian*. Ann Arbor, Mich.: Olivia and Hill Press, 1982.

Baskette, Floyd K.; Sissors, Jack Z.; and Brooks, Brian S. *The Art of Editing*. 4th ed. New York: Macmillan, 1986.

Berner, R. Thomas. *Language Skills for Journalists*. 2d ed. Boston: Houghton Mifflin, 1984.

Bernstein, Theodore M. *The Careful Writer*. New York: Atheneum, 1977.

Bernstein, Theodore M. *Dos, Don'ts & Maybes of English Usage*. New York: Times Books, 1977.

Bernstein, Theodore M. *Miss Thistlebottom's Hobgoblins*. New York: Farrar, Straus and Giroux, 1971.

Bernstein, Theodore M. *Watch Your Language*. New York: Pocket Books, 1965.

Bremner, John B. *Words on Words*. New York: Columbia University Press, 1980.

Brooks, Brian S.; Kennedy, George; Moen, Daryl R.; and Ranly, Don. *News Reporting and Writing*. 3d ed. New York: St. Martin's Press, 1988.

Callihan, E.L. *Grammar for Journalists*. 3d ed. Radnor, Pa.: Chilton, 1979.

Cappon, Rene J. *The Word*. New York: The Associated Press, 1982.

Catalano, Kevin, and Pinson, James. *Editing Manual*. Columbia, Mo.: n.p.: 1987.

Copperud, Roy H. *A Dictionary of Usage and Style*. New York: Hawthorn Books, 1964.

Ehrlich, Eugene, Flexner, Stuart Berg; Carruth, Gorton; and Hawkins, Joyce M. *Oxford American Dictionary*. New York: Oxford University Press, 1980.

Ehrlich, Eugene and Murphy, Daniel. *Schaum's Outline of English Grammar*. New York: McGraw-Hill, 1976.

Finkel, Kenn. *Creative Editing*. 2d ed. Columbia, Mo.: n.p., 1985.

Flesch, Rudolf. *The ABC of Style*. New York: Harper & Row, 1964.

Flesch, Rudolf. *Look It Up*. New York: Harper & Row, 1977

Follett, Wilson. *Modern American Usage: A Guide*. Edited and completed by Jacques Barzun. New York: Hill & Wang, 1966.

Fowler, H.W. *A Dictionary of Modern English Usage*. 2d ed. New York: Oxford University Press, 1965.

French, Christopher W., ed. *The Associated Press Stylebook and Libel Manual*. New York: The Associated Press, 1986.

Gartner, Michael G. Uncollected *Words, Words, Words* columns for the Register-Tribune Syndicate.

Gibson, Martin L. *Editing in the Electronic Era*. 2d ed. Ames, Iowa: Iowa State University Press, 1984.

Gilmore, Gene. *Modern Newspaper Editing*. 3d ed. San Francisco: Boyd & Fraser, 1983.

Gove, Philip Babcock, ed. *Webster's Third New International Dictionary*. Springfield, Mass.: G.&C. Merriam Co., 1986.

Hirsch, E.D., Jr. *Cultural Literacy*. Boston: Houghton Mifflin, 1987.

Hodges, John C., and Whitten, Mary E. *Harbrace College Handbook*. 9th ed. New York: Harcourt Brace Jovanovich, 1984.

Holley, Frederick S. *Los Angeles Times Stylebook*. New York: New American Library, 1981.

Hunter, Estelle B. *A New Self-Teaching Course in Practical English and Effective Speech*. Chicago: The Better Speech Institute of America, 1938.

Jordan, Lewis, ed. *The New York Times Manual of Style and Usage*. New York: Times Books, 1979.

Kennedy, George; Moen, Daryl R.; and Ranly, Don. *The Writing Book*. Englewood Cliffs, N.J.: Prentice-Hall, 1984.

Kesselman-Turkel, Judi, and Peterson, Franklynn. *The Grammar Crammer*. Chicago: Contemporary Books, 1982.

Kessler, Lauren, and McDonald, Duncan. *When Words Collide*. 2d ed. Belmont, Calif.: Wadsworth, 1988.

Kilpatrick, James J. *The Ear Is Human*. Kansas City, Mo.: Andrews, McMeel & Parker, 1985.

Kilpatrick, James J. *The Writer's Art*. Kansas City, Mo.: Andrews, McMeel & Parker, 1984.

Kutie, Rita, and Huffman, Virginia. *The Wiley Office Handbook*. 2d ed. New York: John Wiley & Sons, 1984.

Lewis, Norman. *The New American Dictionary of Good English*. New York: Signet Books, 1987.

Manhard, Stephen J. *The Goof-Proofer*. New York: Macmillan, 1987.

Middendorf, John. *Basic English Grammar & Usage*. Flushing, N.Y.: Data-Guide, 1967.

Miller, Casey, and Swift, Kate. *Handbook of Nonsexist Writing*. 2d ed. New York: Harper & Row, 1988.

Mitchell, Richard. *Less Than Words Can Say*. Boston: Little, Brown, 1979.

Morris, William. *The American Heritage Dictionary*. 2d ed. Boston: Houghton Mifflin, 1982.

Morris, William and Mary. *Harper Dictionary of Contemporary Usage*. 2d ed. New York: Harper & Row, 1985.

Neufeldt, Victoria, and David B. Guralnik, eds. *Webster's New World Dictionary*. 3rd College Ed. New York: Webster's New World, 1988.

Newman, Edwin. *Edwin Newman on Language: Strictly Speaking and A Civil Tongue*. New York: Warner Books, 1980.

Newman, Edwin. *I Must Say*. New York: Warner Books, 1988.

Nunberg, Geoffrey. "The Grammar Wars." *The Atlantic*, December 1983, pp. 31–46.

Pinckert, Robert C. *Pinckert's Practical Grammar*. Cincinnati, Ohio: Writer's Digest Books, 1986.

Prejean, Blanche G., and Danielson, Wayne. *Programed News Style.* 2d ed. Englewood Cliffs, N.J.: Prentice-Hall, 1988.

Quinn, Jim. *American Tongue and Cheek.* New York: Pantheon Books, 1980.

Quinn, Jim. "Hopefully, They Will Shut Up." *Newsweek,* Feb. 23, 1981, p. 9.

Quinn, Jim, "Plain English: How to Stop Worrying and Learn to Love the Language." *The Best of the Post,* edited by Gerald Gross. New York: Popular Library, 1979.

Randall, Bernice. *Webster's New World Guide to Current American Usage.* New York: Webster's New World, 1988.

Ranly, Don. *Grammar & Punctuation for Writers and Editors.* Columbia, Mo.: n.p., 1988.

Research and Education Association. *The English Handbook of Grammar, Style, and Composition.* New York: Research and Education Association, 1984.

Ross-Larson, Bruce. *Edit Yourself.* New York: W.W. Norton & Co., 1982.

Safire, William. *I Stand Corrected.* New York: Times Books, 1984.

Safire, William. *On Language.* New York: Times Books, 1980.

Safire, William. *Take My Word for It.* New York: Times Books, 1986.

Safire, William. *What's the Good Word?* New York: Times Books, 1982.

Safire, William. *You Could Look It Up.* New York: Times Books, 1988.

Shertzer, Margaret. *The Elements of Grammar.* New York: Collier Books, 1986.

Shaw, Harry. *Errors in English.* 2d ed. New York: Barnes & Noble, 1970.

Sledd, James H. *A Short Introduction to English Grammar.* Chicago: Scott, Foresman, 1959.

Sorenson, Sharon. *Everyday Grammar and Usage Simplified and Self-Taught.* New York: Prentice-Hall, 1982.

Strumpf, Michael, and Douglas, Auriel. *Painless, Perfect Grammar.* New York: Monarch Press, 1985.

Strunk, William, Jr., and White, E.B. *The Elements of Style.* 3d ed. New York: Macmillan, 1979.

Temple, Michael. *A Pocket Guide to Correct English.* Woodbury, N.Y.: Barron's Educational Series, 1980.

Walsh, J. Martyn, and Walsh, Anna Kathleen. *Plain English Handbook.* 9th rev. ed. New York: Random House/McCormick-Mathers, 1987.

Webb, Robert A., ed. *The Washington Post Deskbook on Style.* New York: McGraw-Hill, 1978.

Wimer, Arthur, and Brix, Dale. *Workbook for Headwriting and News Editing.* 5th ed. Dubuque, Iowa: Wm. C. Brown, 1983.

Zinsser, William. *On Writing Well.* 3d ed. New York: Harper & Row, 1985.

Zinsser, William. *Writing to Learn.* New York: Harper & Row, 1988.

Index

This index lists the key terms found in the text, as well as misused words receiving special discussion. Thousands of other words that are frequently confused, misused, misspelled and so on, can be found in the appropriate lists referred to here.